Behind the Story of Flight 401 . . .

I cannot ask anyone to really believe some of the things that were to follow. They're out of the realm of believability. The only thing I can say in my defense is that I'm physically strong, mentally awake, and morally straight, as the Boy Scouts put it. John will back me up on these strange events. But his rule during the writing of the *Flight 401* book was not to print anything of a subjective nature, or anything that couldn't be confirmed by outside sources. Therefore, he didn't mention any of these incidents in his book. My rule during the writing of *this* book is to print everything that happened, exactly as it happened.

MY SEARCH FOR
THE GHOST OF FLIGHT 401
ELIZABETH FULLER

MY SEARCH FOR THE GHOST OF FLIGHT 401
ELIZABETH FULLER

With an Epilogue by John G. Fuller,
author of THE GHOST OF FLIGHT 401

A BERKLEY BOOK
published by
BERKLEY PUBLISHING CORPORATION

Aside from my husband, who gave me confidence to write, starting at five in the morning as he did, I'd like to thank Gail Hochman, Elaine Kaufman and Dorothy Thau for their helpful suggestions.

In certain cases, names have been changed on request. These are indicated by an asterisk (*) the first time they are used.

Chapter I

THERE WAS ONE thing that I knew for sure: we lived and we died—and when we died, we were dead. Life after death belonged to fantasy, and fantasy belonged to Disneyland. What then, was I doing in a séance circle? It was my job. I was a part-time research assistant for journalist-writer John G. Fuller. As part of our research we were tracing how a jet-age ghost legend began. However, I never expected to be sitting in a séance circle to do it.

We had arrived late. As I entered the modern office building in Southwest Miami, I felt a tinge of disappointment. Instead of an old mansion, high on a windswept hill, with creaky stairs adorned with cobwebs and bats, I was in a well-lighted building with elevators. There were eight mediums already seated in a circle. The small group looked more like the local PTA than mediums about to communicate with the "other side." There was a banker, a city detective, a housewife, a high school English teacher, a surgical nurse, a sales executive for a large pharmaceutical company, an airline employee, and a college student.

This quiet, conventional group immediately shattered my preconceived image of what mediums should look like. I was convinced that I'd find ladies

1

in turbans, gazing into crystal balls. Still, I couldn't forget how strange the whole idea was. I didn't believe in ghosts, and I certainly didn't believe in spirit communications.

Everyone in the group seemed to be relaxed and cordial. The conversation among them was totally unrelated to the psychic. There seemed to be no levitations or dematerializations in the offing. Everything seemed so normal, I had to keep reminding myself where I was, and what I was there for. The mediums were respectably clad in Miami casual wear, while John and I looked a bit like characters straight off the *African Queen*. John was wearing an Abercrombie's fisherman's hat, a tattersall shirt, minus a button, and khaki trousers that had never met up with an iron. The whole ensemble was topped off with a safari jacket. I looked no better in my jeans, tee shirt, and sandals.

We had arranged the meeting three days beforehand, on the advice of two Eastern Airlines pilots from New York. They were part of a national organization, known as Spiritual Frontiers Fellowship. The organization was created twenty years ago by seventy-five conventional religious leaders from all over the country. They were all from staid and proper denominations. One of their important functions was to investigate the relationship between the paranormal and Christianity. They saw no conflict between the two. The organization had no orthodox creed—except the belief that the dead survive in some not-yet-understood fashion. However, the pilots were careful to emphasize that the group wasn't trying to replace religion—it was a religious supplement.

When John and I made the arrangements by

phone, we were careful not to divulge the exact purpose of our visit. We were researching an alleged story of an Eastern Airlines flight engineer, Don Repo, who had been killed in a 1972 crash in the Everglades. Several months later, crew members and even passengers reported seeing an apparition of the dead flight engineer. The deceased crewman would appear on an L-1011 Whisperliner, a sister ship of the crashed airplane. In several cases the alleged apparition was supposed to have warned that something dangerous was going to happen to the plane. Senior pilots, cabin attendants, and passengers claimed to have had firsthand encounters with the ghost. And three senior pilots had actually "exorcised" the haunted aircraft. The story was not new. It had been bruited about over every airline in the country, even on foreign carriers. Nearly three years later, as we were beginning our research, the stories were circulating more than ever. The Eastern Airlines ghost, Don Repo, was fast becoming a folklore hero.

The key question was: Why were two seasoned pilots introducing us to a group of mediums? And why did these pilots possibly think that these mediums could contact the spirit world? And on top of that, how could we get direct evidential information that could convince us that Don Repo was actually in touch with this world?

Neither John nor I believed this even remotely possible. John was basically working on a story of how a modern myth or legend developed. But as part of our research, we were touching every base. And if that meant séances, that meant séances.

After brief introductions, John slipped past the circle of chairs, and headed straight for the black leather sofa in the corner of the room. I think he was afraid of getting involved. He was muttering something about his credibility. He began his journalistic schtick by inserting a fresh tape into his Sony TC-55, scribbling some cryptic memo in his pocket-sized notebook, all the while casing the spacious room. Meanwhile, I was busy on all fours searching for a socket just in case the Sony power pack needed recharging. Somewhere between the socket and the black sofa, I was intercepted by Patricia Hayes, the leader of the group.

Patricia was a stunning thirty-five-year-old, straw blonde with a healthy glow from the Florida sun. It was hard to believe that she was the mother of five children. It was even harder to believe that she and her husband, Bud, were leaders of a psychic group. They were both such attractive, normal people. After about five minutes of chatting, I was convinced they belonged in the pages of *House and Garden*, not in this offbeat field. Bud, in addition to studying the psychic, had a very successful advertising agency. Patricia, in addition to handling her ménage, had just, belatedly, attained a B.S. degree in behavioral science.

I liked them both, but I couldn't figure either one of them out. Here were two people who seemed to have everything, including wit. They could even relate to how John and I felt about séances. But here were also two people who believed that it was possible to communicate with the dead. I began to ask Patricia questions about the forthcoming séance. Did she really believe it was possible to contact spirits? She wasn't offended. I sensed she wouldn't be, or I wouldn't have been so direct. Her entire expression changed from light amusement to total seriousness.

4

"Yes, of course we believe it's possible to contact the spirit world," she said. "That doesn't mean we advocate any public demonstration of mystical or psychic gimmickry."

Her eyes were intense. She meant what she said. In addition to her extreme good looks, she was persuasive.

"We're aware that often the paranormal can lead to a lot of extremism and self-deception," she said. "So we take a mess of precautions to prevent this kind of thing."

I nodded, but said nothing. If my ears were functioning properly, this lady who appeared so totally sane and rational, actually believed that séances themselves weren't at all extreme. Then she was trying to tell me that that they were taking every precaution to prevent gimmickry. But if what she just said was true—why were they about to sit in a séance circle? I was more baffled than ever.

I felt even more baffled when Patricia asked me to actually join in. Before I could reject the bizarre offer, I was number nine in the circle. I made a final attempt to get John's attention, making subtle gestures with my head and eyes. I was torn. I half-wanted him to come and rescue me, but the other half of me said, *Stay*. I couldn't get his attention anyway. He just sat there fidgeting with his Sony. He was perfectly aware of my predicament. Frankly, I think he was embarrassed by the whole situation.

Patricia Hayes wasted little time in preliminaries. She began by instructing us to all join hands. Then she led us into a prayer, followed by deep-breathing exercises. The breathing was supposed to aid in altering our conscious state to increase our psychic sensitivity. She told us to breathe in peace and exhale love, to send this energy around the circle from the right hand, through the body, and out to the others. We were told to try to imagine our bodies lifting, and every time we imagined ourselves lifting, we were to come back down and mentally imagine that we were taking our partners with us.

I could hear John in the background, clicking the Sony on and off. *It must need recharging,* I thought. *Damn,* I forgot to tell him where the socket was. Well, he'll have to look for it. It was impossible to concentrate; thoughts raced through my mind. The traffic outside was distracting. I wished John would get up and close the window. I should have asked Patricia if there was supposed to be any spirit manifestations. I remembered reading once that that's what happens at a séance. That would really throw John. The camera was out in the car. We should have brought it in. I would try to keep an open mind.

I must have been sitting in the circle for close to ten minutes, but it seemed like hours. Every part of me began to itch. I was in sheer physical agony. I simply couldn't even begin to feel lighter than an armored tank. My mind kept alternating between controlling the desire to scratch, and imagining the expression on my family or friends' faces if they could have seen me huddled between eight full-blooded mediums preparing to conjure up spirits.

Patricia continued to have us breathe in, and hold the breath. With each inhalation, she would gradually increase the length of time we held. We were up to inhaling for a count of eight, holding for a count of eight, and exhaling for a count of eight. At one point I did feel as if I were starting to lift, but it seemed more like a warning symptom for hyper-

6

ventilation, rather than an altered state of consciousness. I was also starting to get a headache.

Just as I began to feel unusually light-headed, I went spinning through my own memories. I thought back to a sixth-grade Halloween party. I had arrived at school decked out as a ghost. As I floated into the classroom, Sister Mary Agnes caught a glimpse of me, and headed toward my desk. She greeted me by making an exaggerated sign of the cross. Then she wrapped her huge hand around the scruff of my neck and went into a five-minute dissertation on why ghosts were not funny. They were not part of the true meaning of Halloween. She told me to get into the girls' room and take off the sheet. I obeyed. Not because I believed that ghosts weren't funny. It was just that Sister Mary Agnes had a powerful left hook. That little scenario did little for my meditative state, but it did confirm what I always knew to be true—there were no such things as ghosts. Sister Mary Agnes had proved it to me.

In spite of Catholic school, I grew up fairly normal. By fairly normal, I mean I had the usual hang-ups you leave Catholic school with: the fear of eternal damnation and Purgatory, an obsession with mortal and venial sins, and so on. I also spent countless hours worrying about all my non-Catholic friends who would never be able to have an eyeball-to-eyeball confrontation with God.

But probably what hung over my head the longest was the dreaded "black patent-leathers." This was Catholic school jargon, and referred to the fact that black patent-leather shoes act as mirrors, and when worn with short skirts, cause pregnancy. Fortunately, today I am able to wear black patent-leather shoes—with slacks.

I was seven years old before I committed my first mortal sin. There was a Lutheran Church behind our playground. To enter any other church was taboo. My best friend dared me to go into the church for the count of 100. I accepted the perilous dare, as long as she promised to stand a respectable distance away, to get help in case I never came out. My knees were trembling as I stood just inside the door. As quickly as I could, I counted to 25, without even coming up for air. I waited for a few seconds and nothing happened. I immediately began to resume my counting, until I hit 75. I paused and looked around. I was still standing. I got to 100, and *nothing happened.* I waited and I waited, and nothing more happened. And then I counted out an additional 100 just to make sure. Still nothing. At that point I knew I wasn't getting the whole story.

Of course, you never get the whole story growing up in an Italian-Irish family in the suburbs of Cleveland. It's not exactly conducive to developing what is now popularly known as "psychic awareness." Our family didn't encourage us to discuss that which you can't see, sex included. As a child I reached my psychic peak in my fifth year. My brother, Gary, was two years older than I. It was about that time we discovered a very interesting phenomenon. If we got up in the middle of the night and immediately looked underneath our beds we could see entire streets and villages, little houses and even trains and trolley cars. It was the most fantastic combination of dust and vivid imaginations ever assembled under two twin beds. We kept up the late-night schedule for what seemed like years, but it was probably only over a period of a week or two—if that. Then one night our miniature city disappeared. My mother had swept underneath the beds.

Patricia's words brought me back to the present, alive and well and in a séance in Miami. "I'm going to ask that you all visualize yourselves surrounded by a spiritual white light," she continued. "This is protection from any evil force that may want to try to influence your bodies."

White lights! This whole thing was beginning to sound like something out of *The Exorcist*, and I didn't believe that either. But I had to admit they were capturing the drama.

She went on to say that once you are able to imagine yourself wrapped in a white light, you should try to imagine the entire group all together in the same light. "Void your mind," she said, "and think of nothing but the brilliant beam, and try to follow it upward...."

Even though I didn't believe in the paranormal and had no idea what a "white light" was supposed to mean, it was still a little spooky to me. The only person I knew who had a direct encounter with it was my father. I had a sneaky suspicion that he may have believed in things like this. Often as a kid around the dinner table, one of us would urge him to tell how "the old lady" cured him. We never got tired of that story. There was a bit of protesting. Everybody always protested everything there was to protest. It was a matter of family policy. But my father would begin:

"When I was a couple of years old they discovered I was an epileptic," he said. "The doctor told your grandmother that I'd grow out of it, but I didn't. By the time I was five years old, the seizures were so frequent they were scared for my life. The doctors said they couldn't do anything more for me, but your grandmother wouldn't listen. She took me all over Cleveland to different specialists. I just got worse. As a last resort Ma took me to the other side of Cleveland to see 'the old lady.'" He would always stop the story at some dramatic point like this to sip his coffee.

Then his voice would soften. "'The old lady' would lay her hands on the top of my head and pray. She wasn't even a Catholic, but Grandma didn't care. She cared about one thing: 'the old lady' was curing me. Your grandmother could feel things about people. She knew if people were good, before she knew them. The entire time, we prayed. I felt like something was happening to me, but I could never explain what. After each visit, my attacks were fewer and fewer. Then one day, about a year later, our visits to the other side of Cleveland stopped. I was cured."

We never knew if he was going to tell the long version of the story or the short version, but we would all sit around feeling eerie, waiting for the time he would pick up his wineglass and say "*Se Dio vuole.*" It was an Italian phrase meaning, "If God wants it." It also meant the story had ended.

Although the tale often varied, his expression never did. Each time he told us about the "miracle healing," he had the same look in his eyes. It was a look that was reserved for "the old lady." It was almost as if to say there are many things we just don't know about. But he would never admit to that. He would admit to only one thing. He knew everything there was to know—and that was that.

To others, my childhood was not very exciting. But I was under every illusion that it was. However, as I grew older I realized that there was more to life than living in a palatial split-level situated on over a quarter of an acre, smack in the middle of suburbia.

It was a custom-designed home, with wall-to-wall, white shag carpeting, and chandeliers hanging everywhere. The focal point was a large black velvet scene of Venice, that even lighted up.

My dream of being a Mouseketeer faded with the stark reality that I would never be able to adequately sing "Meeska-Mooska-Mouseketeer—Mouse Cartoon-Time-Now-Is-Here." I did realize my limitations. I decided on the next best occupation: to be an airline stewardess.

After a two-year stint at Ohio State University, I confirmed what Sister Mary Agnes told me nearly thirteen years earlier. I was not your Basic Scholar. I said goodbye to Columbus, and joined Northwest Orient Airlines. I would go through a five-week training program in Siberia's sister city, Minneapolis, beginning November 17, 1968. My dreams were beginning to materialize. First, Minneapolis. Then the world. Well, maybe not the world to start with. My first year of flying, I was assigned trips that took me to all corners of the Midwest. I was doomed.

The bon-voyage scene at Cleveland Hopkins Airport looked like a presidential send-off. All eight of us arrived in my father's iridescent blue Cadillac. To anybody watching us all pour out of the car, it must have resembled a circus act. Nobody was over 5'7" except Uncle Chris, and he lied. Eight abreast, we all paraded down the concourse, not restraining our dialogue.

My mother was schlepping two grocery bags stuffed with hard salamis, homemade bread, and most of the pantry. I kept telling her that I was almost sure that they had grocery stores in Minneapolis. She wouldn't listen.

My father was carrying Anne, my baby sister

11

who was then two years old. Lewis, my seven-year-old brother, was sprinting up and down the concourse. Gary, the poet, was reciting a sonnet aloud, and my grandmother kept stuffing dollar bills into my pocket.

There was little time for goodbyes. I was grateful for that. It was so confusing. Everybody was talking at the same time. The conversation ranged from my first Holy Communion party fifteen years earlier, to reminding me to put the salami in a cool place. Then there were the traditional hugs, and kisses. I collected the bags and walked quickly to the jetway. I only turned around once—I didn't want them to see the tears rolling down my cheeks.

They were still calling after me to phone next Sunday, and go to church. They stood at the gate, waving as if I were leaving forever. The scene would have been the same whether I was going to Pittsburgh for a week or the slammer for life. We were all very close. Nobody would ever admit it, but we all knew it.

Now, back in Miami, seven years after this family send-off, I was still flying for Northwest Orient. However, things were looking up. I was no longer confined to the Midwest. I had broadened my horizons as far as Tokyo. I had also broadened my interest to include doing free-lance research for John.

It was my second month on the strange hunt for the Ghost of Flight 401. So far, I had collected half a dozen ghost tales from Eastern and other airline crews. I scrawled the strange accounts on my personal stationery—airsick bags. I had also managed to canvas the New York airport lounges and crew-scheduling offices that Northwest shared with Eastern. Needless to say, it was much easier for me to quiz the Eastern crew members about their resident ghost than it was for John. Eastern pilots, as a rule, refused to discuss the ghost stories with anyone outside the airlines.

My first two months as a researcher, I didn't run into any Eastern personnel who actually claimed firsthand encounters with the ghost. But I did hear lots of second- and third-hand stories. My research had barely started and there was a lot more digging to do. At the end of my first two months I made an interesting discovery: of all the crews I interviewed, the stories were basically the same. They didn't shift base as many legends and rumors do.

I was currently flying Miami layovers. I had arrived at the hotel just before six, with barely enough time to change out of my uniform and go over my notes before John arrived. I had declined an invitation to go to the local Mexican restaurant with the rest of the crew.

In fact they were probably getting ready to devour the onchiladas as I was hearing Patricia's voice. It was beginning to sound more distant. Ten minutes must have passed since we began the séance. I was beginning to wonder how long it was going to last.

Suddenly, without warning, I felt weightless. All thoughts blanked out of my mind. That's when it happened. I was *compelled* to talk. It was unlike any feeling I have ever experienced before. Words started to come out of my mouth. I began calling out four names of people, one by one. They were names I had never heard before.

The first name was Christina, an infant.

The man sitting to my right said abruptly: "The baby lives."

Then I said, "I get the name of another baby. It's also named Christina."

The same man said: "This baby lives, too."

I said, "I now get the name of Mrs. Jackson. A Mrs. E. Jackson."

The same man said to me: "She died."

The last name I received was Jacobs. The man next to me said he was alive.

The séance had ended and I was still sitting in the circle. The rest of the group were all talking as if nothing unusual had happened. I looked over at Patricia for some sort of an explanation. But she just looked over at me, as if to say she knew something would happen all the time.

Patricia invited us to stay and have coffee, but I needed some fresh air. I explained that I had an early flight the next day, and that I would be in touch as soon as I digested the strange communication. We left, and on the drive back to my hotel, John asked what the hell had come over me. One thing about John, he didn't mince words. I told him that I couldn't explain what had happened. But I felt as if those names were in some way related to the crash of Eastern's Flight 401.

All I knew for sure was that out of nowhere, those names came to me. I don't know why or where I got them. John was relentless. He kept up his journalistic cross-examinations, and framed the same question about twenty different ways. I was frustrated, and he wasn't helping matters any.

"Come on, Elizabeth, you just don't get names out of nowhere. You're acting like those mediums," he said. "Pretty soon you're going to tell me that you were communicating with spirits." He slammed one hand hard against the steering wheel. "My researcher has flipped out," he sighed.

My first impulse was to knock out his teeth. But my second impulse was to laugh. And that's exactly what we did. We laughed.

It was about 10 P.M. before we arrived back at my hotel in Miami Springs. We decided to have a snack in the coffee shop, while discussing where to go from here. Or if we would go anywhere from here.

Over a grilled cheese sandwich and coffee, we drew up plans for the next day. John would pick me up at 8 A.M. sharp, we would have breakfast, and leave the hotel no later than 8:30. From there, we would go the Miami library where there was a newspaper morgue, and check the *New York Times* and Miami papers for any clues to these mysterious names. I would be back at the hotel in time for my noon flight. I might even have time for a swim before I headed back to Siberia.

I had no trouble falling asleep. The day had been long. The next day would be longer. I drifted off, trying to figure out where those four names came from.

The next thing I knew, the phone was ringing. John was on the other end. "I thought the spirits might have taken you away last night."

"Very funny," I said. "I must have overslept. I'll be right down." As swiftly as I could, I threw on my jeans, grabbed my overstuffed stew bag, and headed for the coffee shop.

We arrived at the library on schedule. The librarian handed John the requested microfilm and gave him instructions on how to use the projector. For

the first time since the séance, I had the same strange
feeling. It was a feeling of knowing something was
happening, but not knowing what. John began to
insert the small roll of film into the machine. I was
feeling sort of sheepish for dragging John to the
library on such a far-out long shot. I couldn't even
adequately explain to him how I connected those
four names to Flight 401, the flight Don Repo was
killed on.

Within seconds, headlines from the microfilmed
New York Times flashed on the screen. There were
two lists: Survivors and Passengers Known or Pre-
sumed Dead.

I pressed my finger to the television-sized screen,
and moved it down alongside the names in tiny
print, first in the Survivor list.

Then I saw it. I looked away for a second to
refocus my eyes. I looked back, and it was still there:
Christina. Christina Casado, aged two months. She
lived. A distinct chill whipped through me. I supposed the whole time I wasn't really prepared to find
a Christina on the list. I immediately began to ra-
tionalize what I saw. It was a coincidence, of course
it was. There could never be two babies named
Christina. My nerves were calmed.

I continued to run my finger down the list. If my
nerves were calmed, my heart wasn't. It was pounding as if I had just run the Boston Marathon. I
couldn't hear any outside noise. At the top of the
next column, still on the Survivor list, the miniature
print spelled out what I couldn't believe. There was
another Christina: Christina Ochoa, one year old.

I immediately checked the first Christina to see if
they had accidentally printed her name twice. They
hadn't. I had a flash of the séance circle, only twelve

hours earlier. The man on my right had said the two babies lived. The paper said the same thing. Did the man surreptitiously get this information ahead of time? No, he couldn't have, because none of the mediums knew ahead of time who we were trying to contact. It was a blind test. Besides, I was the one who came out with the names. Then, did I read somewhere about the two Christinas? I knew that I hadn't seen the passenger list. Could this have been all just a strange coincidence? First the séance, then these two names? I began to think it couldn't be, but I still had two more names to check.

I resumed my search, this time on the bottom of the page. The names were listed in alphabetical order. It would be much quicker to find Jackson and Jacobs. I zeroed right in on the *J*'s. There were six. Sandwiched between Infantino and Jacter was a Jackson. I didn't trust what I read. John confirmed it. It was a Mrs. E. Jackson. She was dead. For the third time the man on my right at the séance had information that was correct.

I would never forget that moment. I felt as if I were in a dream. My vision started to blur. Nothing seemed real. I went back over the names, expecting them to vanish. I thought my eyes were playing tricks on me. They weren't.

The name of Jacobs wasn't on either list. He would turn up later in another paper. Jacobs was a newsman who had covered part of the crash story.

I knew that this was no longer a coincidence. But what I didn't know was that this was the beginning of a whole series of strange events in my life. Stranger than I ever dreamed possible.

Chapter II

I HAD STARTED with no psychic ability, but I was to learn that when it did arrive, it would arrive in bite-sized chunks. My life as a Northwest Orient stewardess before the strange incident at the Miami séance was uncolored by the remotest hint of any psychic awareness: If it had developed earlier, I might have been forewarned of an event that almost cost me my job.

From the start, I had followed the routine of my work in dubiously strict accordance with all the company procedures. Practically every airline has a manual, and Northwest is no exception. There were strict rules about Cabin Attendant conduct, and the wording was never hazy. Usually, these manuals tell us that we must have our personal qualities developed to the highest degree, and that we certainly should have poise, good judgment, diplomacy, courtesy and every other attribute of a model Girl Scout, including a spotless appearance. Usually, these manuals make it clear that the company doesn't want to jump into our private lives, unless of course they feel they have to.

Whenever I looked at myself in the mirror, I would muffle a smirk as I matched myself against these qualities. I had not been an underachiever except maybe during my years at school. Yes, that manual described the real me. Poised. Tactful. Dependable. Adaptable. Packed full of initiative and good judgment. I could also be myself, because the company had no wish to interfere with my personal affairs.

But my personal affairs did overlap with theirs on one memorable flight. It all happened on a routine shuttle from Minneapolis to Washington. By the time we reached Washington that morning for a two-hour layover, I was tired. It was a dreary morning. I wanted to crawl in beside Lincoln at his monument. It was at that point that I lost all my dignity.

For some cosmic reason, my eye caught the overhead rack. The crew had disembarked for a bite to eat. The new passengers had not yet boarded. Two hours stretched out ahead of me. It was an oasis of time to myself. There were all those little pillows up there on the rack, snuggled next to the blankets. I studied the rack. Yes, there *was* space up there, enough to make a tiny bunk and smother myself with blankets.

I piled the pillows up, smoothed out two folded blankets on the base of the rack, and climbed up.

This was not easy in a skirt and my regulation red half-slip. But I did it. And it was *heaven*. I lay back on the mountain of pillows, pulled a blanket up over my head, and within seconds I was in Dream City. Just before I drifted there, the thought crossed my mind that I ought to set my small, portable alarm clock—but it was too late then. I was exquisitely tired and relaxed. It was delicious.

I never really gave our Operations Manual a thought. According to our bible, cabin attendants are not allowed to slumber while on duty, not even an innocent cat nap. If we were caught with our eyes in a down position we would be canned.

Well, maybe I did give it a second thought. But I really, actually wasn't on duty, in the strict sense. What's more, I was reflecting certain attributes most cherished by the Operations Manual. Initiative. Adaptability. Nothing could show more "initiative" than converting an overhead rack into a nirvana. Besides, my being so utterly exhausted was a personal affair, and the manual assured me that the company had no desire to interfere with such, unless forced to. I certainly wasn't going to force them into anything.

I don't know when I had savored such sleep. It was the sleep of the just, obviously, because I felt no restlessness, no swirling thoughts in my head. Just divine, dreamless drowsiness. I don't quite know how the billowy softness of a dreamless sleep can suddenly break into a stark nightmare, even before you've had a chance to knit the raveled sleeve of care. All I know is that I dropped the whole ball of yarn in one fragment of a second.

It was the captain's voice on the PA system. Usually, his voice was quite dulcet. At this precise moment, it was hideous, rasping. Not that his words and voice were really that bad. It was what he was saying:

"Morning, folks. This is your captain speaking. We're number four for takeoff, up near the end of the runway. So if you'll just sit back and relax, we'll be taking off in a few minutes. The girls will do the best they can for you this morning, even though they are one stewardess short in the second cabin. Sorry you'll be a mite inconvenienced, but I know the other girls will make up for it."

That's what he said. That's exactly what he said. I was hanging on to every word. The situation was obvious, even in my foggy condition. We were sitting out near the end of the runway. Fourth in line. The crew had boarded, looked, and found me not. How they missed the overhead rack, I don't know. There was a dereliction of duty here by *someone*.

If they had just checked the rack with their hands, I would have jumped and screamed. But I would have been down there on the cabin floor, with my one-inch grosgrain ribbon in place, my gold logo centered over the tread marker of my hat, free of perspiration and breath odors. Instead, I was up there on that overhead rack, breaking out in a cold sweat, and trying to analyze the situation.

I opened my eyes slowly, even though I wanted to keep them shut. All I could see was the coarse weave of the blanket, which covered my face like the shroud of a corpse. Whatever I did now would prove my mettle. Whatever I did, I would have to reach into the bank of those qualities that the Northwest manual held so dear. Most certainly, I would have to draw on poise, tact, good judgment, and adaptability again. The neat, trim appearance factor would have to go to hell. Initiative would have to be scrapped. I had exhausted my supply of that in climbing up to where I was.

I did some quick figuring. There were three more takeoffs and landings. They'd have to find me sooner or later on that routine. So I couldn't just stay where I was and pretend the whole thing wasn't happening.

I decided to bring initiative back into the picture. I very gingerly peeked out and down, hoping that no passenger would see me and scream.

There it was, below me. The whole damn cabin. Packed. Jam-packed. Three across one side. Then the aisle. Then three across the other side. Cattle. But they were dignified cattle. Not one shopping bag, not one hippie, no babies. Just a ship full of dark pinstripe suits. Some of them Brooks Brothers, some of them Sears. But almost all pinstripes. There was also a small ocean of *Wall Street Journals*. Anyone who wears pinstripe suits and reads the *Wall Street Journal*, I automatically feel intimidated by. Except that this time, intimidation was something I couldn't afford.

So I said to myself, *Just get down. Don't think of how you're going to do it. Just get down there*. There was, I told myself, no graceful way to do it when you're 5'3", and in a skirt and that regulation slip. Not even pettipants. Directly below me were two pinstripes and a black silk double-breasted; two *Wall Street Journals* and a *Dun's Review*. So I took a deep breath, and lowered my left leg first. This snagged the immediate attention of the last ten rows, along with my panty hose. Only panty hose of a conservative shade could be worn with the uniform.

Then I lowered my right leg, and got the first ten rows. By this time, the last-ten-rowers were out of their seats or craning. They weren't laughing. Just looking on in utter disbelief. Pinstripe No. 2 was in the center seat. I was glad it wasn't the slippery Silk Suit No. 1.

I don't quite know how to describe the expression on the face of Pinstripe No. 2 when I stepped on his lap with my plain, navy blue, high-heel pumps. The wool worsted wasn't slippery, and my arch locked neatly above his knee.

Seizing quickly on Poise, Tact, and Friendliness, I explained to him that my hat was in the overhead rack, and I had been digging around for a long time, and I simply couldn't find it. I pointed out as judiciously as I could that I *had* to wear my hat, or I would be sacked.

He did not do much more than mutter—something about "...sacked anyway." I thanked him for his understanding, and went directly to the center galley. There were my two crewmates, doubled over. I tried to tell them that it was no joke. I had really fallen asleep up there.

Suddenly it hit me that *somebody* would have to notify the captain that his stewardess had miraculously turned up on board. Being the coward that I am, I pleaded with one of the other stewardesses to report the news to him. After much cajoling the junior girl acquiesced, removed her smock, and marched forth.

Meanwhile, after mustering up the necessary courage, I put on my smock, and marched back into the cabin and began pouring coffee, trying to avoid the rows near that part of the overhead rack where the pillows were still piled like a prehistoric tomb.

As I was headed back to the galley to refill my coffeepot, I was taken by surprise. The captain was walking toward the galley, and also toward me. He rarely left the cockpit on short hops. This could mean only one thing: he wasn't just stretching.

No words were exchanged. He leaned against the forward bulk of the galley, folded his thickish arms, and said, "Elizabeth, tell me exactly where you were before takeoff, the whole story, word for word."

I did.

"Is that it?" he said.

I had that same sickening feeling that I had while in the overhead rack. "Yes, that's it," I said.

Still glaring at me, he leaned over and yanked the curtain all the way closed. And doubled up.

Someone higher than 30,000 feet was definitely watching over me. But my dignity was short-lived. Apparently, the agent who boarded the passengers in Washington saw me up there, and decided to let me stew in my own juice. After every trip we have to sign in at our home base. As I entered the check-in lounge, they were waiting for me, all five supervisors. The temperature in Minneapolis was a neat 10°. It seemed colder in that office. It was their turn to tell me how much trouble I was in. They kept saying that I was a professional cabin attendant. If I wanted a job as an acrobat, I should have joined the circus. They asked me how did I think it looked to all those passengers to see a Northwest stewardess come tumbling out of an overhead rack with her legs flying in all directions. I was shifty. I tried to change the negative to positive. I started praising Boeing for having such a sturdy, well-built overhead rack.

Anything I said in my defense just stirred up their fury. I was being court-martialed. And the legal fees were high: there was a two-week paycheck fine, and a firm warning that if this happened again I would get a free ticket back to Cleveland. If Sister Mary Agnes had been on that flight, she would have aptly summed up the situation by saying that I was not your Basic Stewardess, any more than I was your Basic Scholar. This was all part of the very un-psychic adventures of being a stewardess.

Many moons and several years after the Great Overhead Rack Incident, I was assigned to Flight 715. It was a trip that would begin in Miami, and end up in Edmonton, Canada. I had not yet begun my psychic research. In fact, I had not yet met John Fuller.

It was a flight like any other flight, as the cliché goes. There were the bourbons, the scotches, the Cokes, the coffee, the little rug rats scampering in the aisle. And always the aroma of burnt entrees permeating the cabin. For the last seven years, my in-flight routine deviated little from this pattern.

Three pilots, two cabin attendants, and I had boarded the Boeing 727 at our home base, Minneapolis. It was the beginning of a three-day trip. We had already met and said our hellos over in the Northwest crew scheduling building, a five-minute bus ride away from the terminal. The starchy antiseptic building looked a little like Rikers Island. It was a necessary meeting place before a trip, as we checked in there before each flight.

As usual, we signed in twice, once on the first floor with the scheduler, and once on the third floor. The third floor is where the supervisors have their offices. And it is also where the cabin attendants have *their* offices: a three-inch slot for company mail. As we signed our names and company numbers in the large loose-leaf book that lay on top of the check-in desk, I always felt as if I were being eyed. And that's because I was. There was somebody permanently assigned to sit at the desk and make sure you were in full regalia. Ever since the discrimination laws were set into motion several years ago, the company has relaxed its more stringent requirements. As a result all the scales have been scrapped. No longer can a supervisor tell you to lay off the Hershey bars. However, if you are so overweight that you are a hazard during an emergency evacuation, they can ground you. But, even if they can't get you on weight, there are still lists of regulations as long as a 747 to abide by. Lists that include everything from gold buckles on your shoes to specified shades of nail polish. But the supervisors were usually fair, even if reluctant about being so.

I had known the other two cabin attendants from previous flights. We had all hit it off, and that meant the trip would go just that much smoother, and faster, too.

I had been flying the longest; therefore, I was senior. As the senior attendant, I had the responsibility of making sure that the in-flight service went as dictated to us in our manual. Being senior also meant that I would work the first-class cabin.

My pre-takeoff duties ranged from making sure that all the cabin's emergency equipment was intact to the more glamorous aspect of the job: making sure the biffies were smelling with rose-scented disinfectant, and counting the liquor and meals, checking them off against the passenger list. Often a passenger would request a special meal, such as vegetarian or kosher, and often the caterers hadn't boarded it.

Flight 715 originated in Miami and had already made two stops before we got on at Minneapolis. Northwest Orient had the only direct flight from Miami to Edmonton. It wasn't exactly a run that other airlines—or, for that matter, crew members—fight to get. I had accidentally made a mistake when I was bidding, and instead of getting my usual run to Tokyo via Honolulu, I would end up flying to Edmonton all month.

Not that Edmonton is all that bad, but in March,

it was a hostage to the polar winds. However, I gracefully accepted both my destiny and my destination philosophically. Several years ago I had vowed that as long as I continued to fly, I would never allow myself to get upset over a crummy schedule. Even if that meant freezing to death in Edmonton. On too many mornings I came out to the airport expecting to be lying on the beaches of Waikiki that same afternoon—only to find myself in Fargo, North Dakota, for the weekend.

Our flight was an hour or so en route. All three of us attendants clustered in the galley, trying to get the liquor service completed, so that we could get on with the meal. That's about the time I heard the other two stews talking about a writer in the tourist-class section. He was researching, of all things, the reports of the Eastern Airlines ghost, and he seemed serious about it.

The subject of the Eastern ghost was certainly not something new. It came up on nearly every trip. I had personally heard several different versions of the ghost tales. In fact, the stories had been circulating on all the airlines for about two years. I didn't believe that the legends were true, but we all found them good conversation pieces.

After I completed my first-class service, I went back to see if the other girls needed any help. They did. I picked up our undistinguished California champagne and began pouring it in the second cabin. Just as I got near the last row, I nearly tripped over a pair of large desert boots that were topped by a pair of long-legged corduroy trousers. Long Legs immediately began apologizing for being so careless as to let the feet dangle in the narrow aisle. Then he mumbled something about the seating area being only large enough for gnomes and small children.

I knew instinctively that this was the guy who was writing about the ghost. I wasn't using ESP either. After about a year of flying, any Cabin Attendant can easily write a complete profile of a passenger just by observing the way he's dressed.

The top half of this one had on a Harris tweed jacket. His graying hair was touching the collar of his blue oxford button-down. His hair was too long for an IBM executive, but too short for a mad professor type. My mental computer immediately punched up a description: a moderately seedy advertisement for Brooks Brothers. He didn't really look like the type who would believe in ghosts. I always associated ghost hunters with the Leonard Nimoy type. I would have thought his interest lay more in mathematical equations, or things like that.

While filling up his small plastic wineglass, I asked, "You the writer?"

He slid his glasses down to the very tip of his nose, looked up, and said, "You the stewardess?"

I was never good at quick retorts. I should have expected such a remark. After all, writers are supposed to always have quick access to clever comments, or they wouldn't be writers...or at least that's what I thought at the time.

"You the guy who's chasing ghosts?" I said.

Removing his glasses altogether and placing them in his pocket, he said, "Nope, I'm not chasing them; but I am chasing how this jet-age legend got started."

We began talking. I discovered that I had even read one of his books. It was called *The Interrupted Journey*. It was an incredible story of a couple named Betty and Barney Hill who while driving home one night through the White Mountains of New Hampshire sighted a UFO. They apparently went into it at the time. When they arrived home, Barney found inexplicable scuff marks on the tips of his shoes; Betty noted rows of mysterious shiny circles on the trunk of their car. And neither could account for almost two hours of their time on the road.

After many months of distress, the Hills had sought medical help from a distinguished Boston psychiatrist and neurologist. Under time-regression hypnosis, the Hills gave almost identical accounts of what had happened during the lost two hours of their journey—a period of time their conscious minds had repressed. It was a strange story.

I asked the writer if he believed in UFOs, and suddenly he became very defensive. He began going on about how he was a journalist who just reported stories. And most of them very straightforwardly. I said that he must have a personal feeling about Betty and Barney, although I remembered that in the book he was careful to not make a commitment.

He said, "Yes I do, but then again, I don't know." I really couldn't figure out what he said. It was at that point that he told me that he was on his way to Edmonton for a TV taping with Betty Hill and Dr. J. Allan Hynek, who was the head of Astronomy Department at Northwestern. And very respectable, too, thank you, he said. He said that if I were really intrigued by the strange case, I could join them all for dinner that evening, and then come to my own conclusion after meeting with Betty Hill. The upshot of our conversation was that they would all pick me up at my hotel at 7 P.M. for dinner.

They did, and it was in grand style. A big, black

Cadillac limousine pulled up in front of the Mc-
Donald House Hotel. I was hoping some of the crew
would see me slip into the long car. It contained only
Betty Hill, John, and myself. The chauffeur drove
us to the posh restaurant where we met with the staff
from the TV station. It was a far cry from where I
was supposed to be going with the rest of my crew.

An evening out with the pilots is always one of
four things. First, there is debriefing in their room
(Airline Code). What it really means, though no one
acknowledges it while you're going up in a crowded
elevator, is having a beer, and listening to tales of
their days in the service as flying aces.

Next choice is dinner at Luigi's Italian restaurant. In every city there is always a Luigi's, and it's
always cheap. That's an eternal truth that never
changes.

Third choice is a movie. It's always about World
War II pilots. And you might as well offer to sit
through the cartoons twice, because you're going to
do it anyway.

Last choice, if indeed these events can be called
choices, is a walk through the city.

But right now, I wasn't at Luigi's. I was in a
restaurant with a real tablecloth and wine bottles
with labels. I had ordered the house special,
Saumon Archiduc, salmon in a sherry-and-cream
sauce.

During the dinner, Betty Hill touched lightly on
her incredible encounter, but mostly she was talking
about her full-time occupation as a senior social
worker in Portsmouth. I was a little disappointed.
She seemed like such an average-type person. The
kind I ran into every day flying. She was so convinc-
ing when she told her UFO story that I couldn't help

31

but believe her. At least I believed she believed it really happened. It was just something that if you don't experience yourself, even if you want desperately to believe the person, it's awfully difficult.

Over the dessert of chocolate mousse, John and I talked at length about the problems of researching a ghost legend. He said that the biggest obstacle to overcome was the crew members' fear of opening up to a journalist.

I told him that although I didn't know a thing about ghosts or any other aspect of the psychic realm, I liked detective work and maybe I could be of some help. I also told him that Northwest shared some of Eastern's ramps and lounges in the New York area, and that I could snoop around easier than he could. Pilots and stews would be more open with a fellow crew member than with a journalist.

My offer took him by surprise. I'm sure he thought it was just a frivolous, spontaneous offer, and that tomorrow morning my enthusiasm would disappear.

I sensed he was weighing the possibility. Then he turned toward me and said that he liked the idea. Our conversation suddenly took on a more serious tone.

I could tell he was teetering back and forth on whether he should even try the Eastern ghost story. He had so many doubts about it. But at the same time, he was convinced that where there was so much smoke, there had to be fire, or at least a spark. He was in the middle of researching a documentary for the U.S. Information Agency, and had so little time. On the other hand, if I could take on an 007 assignment, it might help him decide if there was enough material for a book.

Even if it was only to be a story on how a modern legend got started, John was very thorough in his investigation. He said he would write out a rough assignment list, and leave it at the desk of my hotel.

The next morning I picked up the list from the reception desk. At that very moment the hotel became alive with mystery and intrigue. I felt as if I had secret documents and special devices sewn into my uniform. As I reached the hotel entrance I could almost see James Bond's old Continental Bentley with the "R"-type chassis waiting for me to slide in. My little fantasy ended abruptly as we all piled into the airport limousine that hauled us back to the airport.

Flight 458, a milk run that would eventually end up in Detroit, was just lifting off the runway when I reached underneath my jump seat and plucked out of my flight bag the assignment list John had given me. For a preliminary research assignment, it read like a thesis:

1. This story is so consistent among all the airlines, I'm curious as to why it stays that way. In talking to other crew members in any airlines, try to find out why it doesn't shift. Why is it always Eastern, instead of shifting to other airlines? Why is it always an L-1011? Why is it Don Repo instead of the other crew members of Flight 401? Why do so many crew members take it seriously? I don't expect you to be able to answer all these questions, but anything you could get on them would be appreciated.

2. Interview as many Eastern crew members

33

at those airports where Northwest shares the Eastern ramps or crew lounges. Because there seems to be only a small number of cases, it will be hard to find those with direct experience of whatever the phenomena are. Eastern has something like 8,000 flight attendants and 2,000 or so pilots, so it's not going to be easy.

3. Can you visit an L-1011 and describe the lower galley, elevators, etc.?

4. If you get a chance, can you look up any books on parapsychology dealing seriously and academically with the theory of apparitions. No ghost stories, please. I understand that the British and American Societies of Psychical Research have seriously probed this area in detail at one time or another.

5. For any story that goes beyond conventional borders like this, the research has to be even more painstaking than for a straight story. It also has to be understated. I just don't see how this story can be possible, but it might be interesting to examine the reasons behind it, etc.

6. Keep track of time and expenses. Bill me at $6.00 per hour.

7. Have a nice trip back. Ghostly good wishes for some successful research—

John Fuller

What I was about to embark on was more than just an interesting research project. I had no idea at the time that I would become personally involved with a series of such strange incidents—incidents that would make me think far beyond Northwest or Eastern Airlines—or the research job I had just accepted.

Chapter III

THREE MONTHS HAD passed since I last saw John. I
had sent him some material, although I hadn't been
able to do as much research as I would have liked.
There were reasons.

For some time, my husband and I had been
having problems. Our marriage had been suffering
from the long absences required by my job. The
situation was compounded by the hectic schedule of
commuting 2,000 miles to work, two or three times a
month. Our house was in Northern California. My
base was in Minneapolis, or MSP as the airline
luggage tags put it. In addition, my husband's work
required him to travel all over the world, and to live
in other cities, sometimes for months on end. We
rarely saw each other. When I was home, he often
had to be away, and vice versa.

Our lengthy separations had turned us into
strangers. When we did get together, we shared one
thing: discussion of and planning for the future. We
did nothing to protect the present. All of the little
problems that arose would all be corrected some-
time tomorrow. It would be a time when I would
quit flying and he would have achieved more finan-
cial security. Life in the present had stagnated, and
we didn't even know it. Until one day, when we both

realized that we were two different people, with future plans and dreams that weren't even important to us anymore. We had no present and we had no future. At that point, we knew that we would never be the couple in the Geritol commercial.

In June of 1975, we separated. I left our home in California and moved back to Minneapolis where I had started out seven years earlier.

Even though we parted friends, I felt terrible guilt. For many months I kept going over in my mind each year of our marriage, trying to pinpoint exactly when it had begun to fail. We were caught between the modern attitudes of the "Today People" and the Catholic Church syndrome. Both of us were Catholic and both of us had every intention of living up to the 2,000-year-old traditions of the Church. Divorce to Catholics lies somewhere between the hardcore criminal act and the mildly demented folly. As a child, I never once heard my parents say the word divorce. They always spelled it out. I was the only kid on the block who jumped rope to D-I-V-O-R-C-E-E-E-E-E in rhythm.

I had postponed the time when I would have to tell my family. I told my friends first. I was sure that it would come as a big shock to everyone. When the time came, nine out of ten times, I heard, "Oh, I could have told you that." Or, "I saw it coming." There was no shock or even surprise. I always wondered if they had some sort of mystical insight, or maybe the involved parties are always the last to know.

My parents would be different. They were brought up in practically Victorian ways. You stayed married until death-do-you-part. My mother might be somewhat understanding, but my father would never accept it. If you had a husband who didn't beat, cheat, or drink, you had yourself one helluva man. I held off calling the folks as long as I could. I'll never forget the day I laid the bad news on them. I felt like a criminal. Regardless of how old I was and how long I had lived away from them, whenever I dialed the phone it was as if I slipped through a time warp. Chronologically, I was twenty-eight. Emotionally, I was twelve.

I predicted what they would say to me. It would be the same old pat phrases that they trotted out and adapted for the occasion. "Where did we go wrong?" Or, "God knows, *I've* tried. Your *father's* tried. We've *all* tried."

But this time, it was different. If the phone had had eyes, I could have seen their disappointment. As it was, I could feel their hurt. There was a long pause. Then they said, "Don't worry about a thing. Those things happen." They reminded me of the new house they were building. I could have the room over the garage, with my own private entrance. It would be like having my own apartment.

They had transcended their values, the Church's dogma, and what the relatives and friends would think. They accepted something that they could never really understand. Again, I was their kid, regardless of my mortal sin.

It was summertime in Siberia, Minnesota. I had kept up my slow but steady research. I hadn't heard from John in regard to the airsick bags, so I wasn't sure if he was still planning to do the Eastern ghost story. But I decided to write him a detailed account of my findings, just in case.

Elizabeth Fuller

Dear John:

Hope you received the barf bags. I was going to transcribe the notes, but I thought you might enjoy seeing them in their original form. Maybe I was wrong?

I don't know if you still intend to write the story, but in any event I have dug up some additional material that you might find interesting.

Sorry for not getting to you sooner, but my schedule has been pretty hectic. However, I uncovered an interesting story from an Eastern co-pilot whom I met in the Newark airport. That's one of the places where Northwest and Eastern share facilities. He said that this is the latest rumor that has been floating around. Incidentally, he flies the L-1011s:

According to an L-1011 log book, a flight attendant was in the lower galley of ship No. 318 and saw the apparition of Don Repo. She called down another stewardess who confirmed the apparition. They both called down the flight engineer of the flight, who not only saw the image but talked with him. The "ghost" engineer said to watch out for an engine fire on the plane, and disappeared.

No trouble developed until the last leg of the flight, when No. 3 engine failed. I think it failed at the ramp, I'm not sure. The crew requested permission to ferry the empty plane back for maintenance repair, on two engines. On takeoff No. 3 engine backfired and stalled at an altitude of about 50 feet. The ferry crew shut down the engine, and miraculously were able to make a safe landing on just one engine.

Here's rumor No. 2:

An executive for Eastern boarded an L-1011. He found an Eastern pilot in one of the first-class seats. The pilot looked up at the executive and said he was part of the crew of Flight 401. The startled V.I.P. went up to the cockpit to get the captain, and when they both returned the other pilot had disappeared.

John, don't these two stories coincide almost exactly with what you told me in Edmonton? This Eastern guy would have given me a lot more stories, but as it was I nearly missed boarding. Anyway, he said it's okay to call him. But of course, he asks only one thing—keep his name under your typewriter.

Several days ago an Eastern flight attendant was deadheading on my flight. She didn't have any new stories, but she did have a rather interesting theory. I thought it might be worth passing on.

She said that since Eastern had removed all the salvaged parts from the "haunted" galley of that L-1011 I mentioned above, the ghost of Don Repo had disappeared. Again, I think you mentioned this to me, but I'm not sure.

I personally don't think Eastern would go to all that trouble and expense just because of ghost reports—unless they know something we don't. Anyway, this Eastern stew has my address, just in case she runs across any interesting tidbits. I also have her name and phone number—she's based in Miami.

John, I honestly don't know what to make of all this. Practically every crew member I have run into, Eastern or not, has at least heard of the Eastern ghost. Personally, I can accept Betty Hill's UFO story a lot easier. Please let me know if you want me to pursue "Casper."

Incidentally, I have a friend who is an Eastern ramp agent in Newark, and I'll ask him if he'll take me aboard an L-1011 and check out their galley. Probably next trip in Newark.

Best,
Elizabeth

Several days after I mailed John that letter, I received a phone call from the Eastern stewardess who had deadheaded on my trip a week earlier. Although we had exchanged names and numbers, the call still came as a surprise.

She told me that she had just been assigned an L-1011 trip, and it happened to be that same ship with the strange goings-on in its galley. She began discussing the ghost stories with the other flight attendants, and discovered that one of the girls on her trip had a direct encounter with the ghost. She said that she couldn't give me her name, because the stew didn't want to take any chances of being sent to the company shrink. But she did tell me the whole story, and again her encounter coincided with other reports that I had collected.

I could tell from the tone of her voice that she was very serious. Besides, I couldn't figure out why she would waste the long-distance phone call on a hoax. She didn't even believe in ghosts. The flight attendant was just keeping her promise to let me know if she ran into anything unusual.

That phone call triggered my next move. It

wasn't because of what she had told me, as much as why so many people thought they were seeing ghosts. There must be, I felt, a logical explanation for their strange sightings. I decided to follow step No. 4 on my research list: Go to the library and dig out some books on parapsychology. It was time I discovered the theory behind what I was chasing. At this point, I realized that my research had turned a corner. It was no longer just for John. It was as much to satisfy my own growing curiosity.

When I went to the library, I couldn't believe the size of their collection of books on parapsychology. I sifted through dozens of titles and ended up checking out what appeared to be the most serious.

I was into my second book, *Survival of Death*, by Paul Beard, when I received John's reply.

Dear Elizabeth:

Many thanks for the barf bags. They are almost suitable for framing. The information is very interesting, and backs up many of the things I've been running into down here in Miami, where I'm still working on the oceanography film.

I've been so busy, I haven't had time to dig into the background of all this as much as I'd like to. The story is so incredible that I'm still on the fence about going ahead with it. It's so much easier to deal with tangibles like sharks, fish, seaweed, and continental shelves. On the other hand, suppose this ghost story does become manageable? It deals with the most important story of all—is life continuous? If it is, it's ancient history, but with an up-to-date news break.

Elizabeth Fuller

What has piqued my interest is that I've run into several people down here who have put a new light on the subject. One of them is J.R. Worden, a very sensible guy with a technical background, and a friend of his, Rachelle Faul, who has been studying journalism and is a very bright researcher. I have asked them to do some preliminary research on the same basis as you are doing (I'm going to go broke before I even decide to do this book), and they have come up with some very interesting information.

I haven't got time to go into detail right now, but what it boils down to is that (a) they are both serious students of parapsychology, (b) they are convinced that there is very serious evidence of life after death, (c) they are equally convinced that there is communications via mediums, (d) they know of two Eastern pilots who often have Miami layovers, who are also very deeply interested in parapsychology. The pilots have actually held what they call a "soul rescue" session to lead the spirit of Don Repo on to his spiritual development. It's sort of like an exorcism, I guess, and I'm digging into more facts about it. I don't know what's going on here. I hope I'm not heading for the Laughing Academy.

The theory seems to be that if it's true that we continue after death, we simply go through another door and pick up where we left off. There's a lot of literature on the subject in the *Journal of the British Society for Psychical Research*, and its American counterpart. Both of these organizations include many scientists and they are not in any way the spook-and-kook sort of thing, which I definitely want to avoid. There is also a lot of serious inquiry into the theory of ghosts or apparitions, poltergeists, etc. Again, I swear I haven't gone around the bend.

J.R. Worden and Rachelle belong to a couple of psychic study groups down here, and they feel that it might even be possible to explore the reality of the story through reliable mediums they know. The two pilots are mediums. They believe the subject is anything but nonsense, and one that has a long record of scientific interest in spite of the prejudice against it in some quarters.

Believe it or not, there is also an FAA regional executive from Atlanta who is a medium and serious researcher in the field, and another Eastern pilot from Boston who is said to have conducted another "soul rescue" for Don Repo, entirely independent of the other two pilots. There is also a study group involving several people from another airline.

I've already interviewed the two N.Y. pilots, and they are really serious. I can set up a meeting with the Boston pilot anytime you might be scheduling a layover there. Maybe he would be more open with an airline crew member at hand. Would you let me know? I don't know what to make of all this, either. I still hope I'm wrapped tight.

Let me know if you have a Boston layover coming up, and thanks again for the barf bags.

Confidently,
General Custer

P.S.: Yes—please pursue "Casper." And
where is your bill?

It was midsummer before I was able to get a
Boston layover. I was excited about the prospect of
meeting with the flight engineer, but at the same
time, I had some anxieties. All the while I was
interviewing crew members, I hadn't been able to
get a single account of a direct firsthand encounter.
After several months of research, I was fairly certain
that the "exorcisms" were merely rumors that somehow got circulated.

But when John wrote and said he had already
talked to two pilots and would be setting up an
appointment with another, that meant maybe there
was more to the story than I ever dreamed possible.
Or was it that General Custer wasn't wrapped too
tight, regardless of his claims?

But I doubted that. I had read two of his books
since that evening in Edmonton: *Fever: The Hunt
for a New Killer Virus*, and *The Day of St.
Anthony's Fire*. They were both scientific detective
stories, and not at all suggestive of any far-out theory. They were pragmatic and down-to-earth. One
of them had won a prize from the New York Academy of Sciences, and both had been Literary Guild
choices, according to the librarian. I knew he was a
reputable author, in spite of the unusual story we
were pursuing, even without his reminding.

Even before I received John's letter I was slowly
beginning to feel that maybe there was a lot more to
our existence than meets the eye. I came to this
conclusion after reading several serious books and
studies on parapsychology. I no longer doubted that
there were certain people who could pick up mes-

sages telepathically, bend metal, or even perform telekinesis—that is, move objects with the mind. I realized for the first time that our brain is the most powerful computer in the world, and it is only working at a fraction of its capacity. I also learned that psychics were being studied by chemists and physicists and psychiatrists at world-famous universities. And I found I was behind the times in not knowing this to begin with.

This new enlightenment came after many hours of poring over books stuffed into my flight bag. Still, all the books in the world could never convince me that ghosts were a real phenomenon. In my limited survey, ghosts just didn't wash. Nor could I go for the life-after-death bit.

Even without belief in ghosts, I was opening up to a whole new world of interesting discoveries. I was beginning to feel that just because you don't believe in one facet of the paranormal, that doesn't automatically make the rest of the field incredible. That would be the same as saying: Toadstools are poisonous; therefore, all mushrooms are poisonous. You can pick and choose. I chose not to believe in ghosts.

The meeting was set. I was on my way to Boston to meet with John, the flight engineer, and his wife. John had phoned the night before, making last-minute plans as to where we would meet. We talked about some of the key points he wanted to discuss with the engineer. John knew very little about Dick Manning,* other than the fact he had conducted some sort of an exorcism on the ship with the weird galley incident at about the same time the two pilots in New York performed their "soul rescue." John felt that what made it so interesting was that the pilots in New York had no idea that the flight engineer in Boston was doing a parallel soul rescue and vice versa.

John had also mentioned that Dick had had some reservations about meeting with us, but he had reassured the engineer that nothing would be put into print unless it was mutually agreed upon. And of course, his name would be changed.

John, Dick Manning, and Dick's wife were all waiting for me in the lobby of the Boston-Sheraton. I had no idea of what to expect. I hadn't yet read anything about mediumship. I was still plowing through a book called *Modern Experiments in Telepathy*, and still getting used to the idea of ESP. I expected the worst; at the very least, a cape, top hat, and a vessel of holy water. But there were no weird clothes. Dick was wearing a light-blue leisure suit. His wife was wearing a dark, tailored pantsuit. They were both in their thirties and looked as if Central Casting had picked them for the roles of the people next door.

John had been talking with the couple for nearly half an hour before I arrived. Accordingly, when I walked into the hotel, there was none of the tension that I had anticipated.

Over lunch, we listened while Dick told us how he first heard of the ghost, up until the time he performed what he described as a "deliverance."

Dick was a well-versed student of the Bible. He believed that ghosts were scripturally correct, and he claimed to have consoled several stewardesses by reassuring them of this.

Finally, one night in an attempt to end the misty appearances, he entered the lower galley of the L-1011 ship and performed the "deliverance."

He believed that he was delivering the spirit of Don Repo from his earthbound anguish, and that he was helping him achieve spiritual development. Or at least, that's how he put it. Dick explained the theory behind earthbound spirits. In the case of sudden accident, the person involved hasn't had time to prepare for his passing over. And consequently, the spirit doesn't know that he is dead. He said that all he is really doing is trying to help the person realize that he is no longer on the earth level and guide him to his rightful place.

The lunch lasted for several hours. When Dick was telling us of his "deliverance," John kept filtering in every imaginable question. "Exactly what did you see when you went into the lower galley? How can you be sure that what you saw was the spirit of Don Repo? Did anybody else see it? Can you remember the exact time it took to perform the deliverance? How can you be sure the galley turned icy? Where were the other flight attendants while you were doing this? Can you reconstruct your dialogue with the other flight attendants?" There were many other questions.

I felt slightly embarrassed for Dick. John was really grilling him. All that was missing was the spotlight glaring into his eyes. I was more subtle. I kept looking into Dick's eyes. It was an old trick that I picked up from watching *Dragnet*. The theory is that if the pupil dilates—the person is lying. Dick's pupils didn't dilate, if that meant anything.

Even though I couldn't relate to what Dick was talking about, I felt he was sincere in his beliefs. He had an uncanny knack for hooking words together so that his sentences came out sounding almost logical. But all the logic in the world could not convince me that what these people were seeing was a ghost.

After the Mannings had left, John and I sat in the lobby and talked. Neither one of us wanted to voice an opinion, but I broke the ice.

"You believe that guy?" I said.

"I believe he really performed that deliverance, or whatever he called it," John said.

"Yeah, I believe he really did it, too. But do you believe all that about the ice appearing in the galley and the spirit of Repo forming and lights flickering?"

"Do you mean, do I believe that he actually saw the spirit of Don Repo?" John said. "I believe *he* believes it."

"What about that stewardess you started to tell me about last night?" I asked. "The one who actually saw the head of Don Repo forming in the galley. Is she one of the flight attendants who talked to Manning?"

"You mean Ginny Packard*?" John said. "I called her several weeks ago. She confirmed that she had talked to Manning. And that he had reassured her she wasn't nuts."

"Is Ginny the one who reported the sighting to her supervisor, and the supervisor suggested she see the company shrink?"

"She's one of them," John said. "There were several. Anyway—I've just decided to go ahead with the research. There's gotta be something here."

"John, that's admitting that you believe him, isn't it?"

"No, I'm just saying that there's something here."

"Like what?" I questioned.

"Like a lot more research."

"John, do you realize that if Manning did see the spirit of Repo, then maybe there *is* a lot more out there?"

I thought back to my Catholic youth. As a child, I had believed in life after death. So many years I spent beating the beads, praying for all the poor souls in Purgatory, praying for all the sinners in the world. I prayed for everybody and everything. Then when I ran out of things to pray for, I did my homework. But I grew up. I stopped praying. I realized that life after death was just a nice fairy tale that helps you to accept the inevitable.

John said, "It would be an important story: does life continue? But I just don't want to write a Nancy Drew spook story."

I asked John if he believed in life after death.

He said that he'd like to see some more proof.

He couldn't be sure. He had never been able to fully accept the Bible, even though he had been half-Presbyterian, and half-Quaker. He liked the Quakers, because they left the question open. "But," he said, "right now, I don't see how it's possible. I'm just keeping an open mind."

"Well," I said. "As long as we agree on that point, where do we go from here?"

"Well," John said. "We could try a séance."

"A what?"

"A séance," John repeated.

"And talk to spirits? That type of séance?"

"Is there any other kind?" he answered.

I couldn't believe what I had just heard. It was so out of character for John to want to go to a séance.

"Where did you ever get that idea?" I said.

"From the two pilots I interviewed in New York."

"The ones who performed the soul rescue?" I asked.

"Yeah, they suggested that if I wanted some factual information from people not involved directly with the apparition, I should go to a séance," he said. "But I was holding off until I met with Manning and heard his story before I decided."

"But I thought you didn't believe Manning," I said. "I'm really confused now."

"Let me put it this way," John answered. "I wasn't convinced by Manning any more than I was by the other two pilots from New York. But when you put all the stories together, and weigh the evidence, there is something *there*." Then he paused a moment. "I think," he added.

"Then you believe all three of them?"

"I didn't say that."

"Well, what did you say?"

"I said that there is something there."

Once again, I didn't quite know what he said, or what he meant.

John went on to tell me about the Spiritual Frontiers group in Miami, and about Patricia and Bud Hayes. It was at this time that we arranged for that memorable séance in Miami, where those names had come to me so inexplicably. The whole thing happened so suddenly, I barely had time to catch my breath. By the time the séance had finished, and we had confirmed the names in the newspaper files the following day, neither of us were sure where we were going to head next. If we had known just how involved the research would become, I don't know if we would have decided to carry on.

Chapter IV

THE SEQUENCE OF events had brought us to visit the Mannings in Boston, then had moved us on to the Miami séance. The things that had happened at that séance had caused a 7.0 Richter-scale shock to my belief system, according to my built-in seismograph.

The spontaneous information on 401's passengers that had come through that night seemed to have been derived from some big computer in the sky. I had been convinced it wasn't a trick of memory or the subconscious. I had wondered if the research on the illusory Ghost of Flight 401 was not going to turn into a search for some kind of truth that had eluded me up to this point. I was determined, however, to keep both navy blue pumps on the ground, even when I was 30,000 feet in the air.

Some things are contagious. I couldn't help but notice that as we went along John was getting increasingly interested in this strange set of circumstances. At regular intervals we both kept checking to make sure that our enthusiasm was not rubbing off on each other and causing us to lose our objectivity.

Our next step after that Miami séance was to visit three more mediums. I had bid a New York layover just for the occasion. John picked me up at La Guardia and we drove to an old brownstone.

John and I sat down in Laura Britebarth's* Manhattan living room, along with Stan* and Carol Chambers.* All three were Eastern employees. All three were mediums. Stan and Carol, along with the another pilot and his wife, had performed what they called a soul rescue in May 1974. John had mentioned this to me in his letter. I wanted to know more about it.

Laura was an Eastern ticketing agent, in her mid-twenties and very attractive. Her home looked about as much like a medium's as my supervisor's office. Scattered throughout the contemporary, one-bedroom apartment were curios from all over the world. Among the more exotic pieces were an elaborately carved primitive Nigerian sculpture, large Indian batik wall hangings, and a stark Peruvian rug that was her latest acquisition.

Stan and Carol were in their early forties, although they appeared more youthful. Like Laura, they were warm and lively. There were absolutely no telltale signs of mediumship anywhere, but by now I was beginning to wonder if a medium were different from anybody else.

John had met them all several times before in his preliminary research. He was somewhat impressed with the threesome, and was anxious to have me meet them. I also think he wanted a second opinion. I was glad for the opportunity. I wanted to check things out myself.

At the time I had met the Mannings, in Boston, I had been bewildered, at the very least. All this was pretty heavy. The same with the Miami séance. I had many questions that were left unanswered. But since that time, I had been reading a lot on the theory of apparitions and life after death. I began to realize that all this wasn't as illogical and strange as I once believed. I was finding out things. There were intelligent people who took this sort of thing seriously. I was a little astonished to learn that the British Society of Psychical Research had made lengthy surveys of apparitions. They found that such appearances were not only possible, but probable. One study showed that 20 percent of 30,000 people surveyed reported they had seen apparitions at one time or another. Many of the appearances corresponded to the exact time the death of a loved one occurred in some distant place. The British studies also indicated that apparitions were often associated with a crisis situation, and that what appeared could be a solid, well-dressed citizen, just as in life. Weird, I was thinking as I studied the survey.

But this seemed to be in keeping with the Don Repo appearances. He had been in a crisis situation. Oftentimes, Repo appeared to deliver a warning that something harmful was going to happen to the L-1011. I thought back to the incident, when Repo was reported to have warned of a fire in an engine. Maybe the crew members had really seen what they claimed to have seen. And if it turned out that they had, then this was the whole guts of the story: Was Don Repo living in another realm of existence?

The amount of books and other material in the library on the subject of life after death was staggering. I knew I wouldn't be able to get through a fraction of it. My brief "007" research so far did indicate that scientists like Sir Oliver Lodge and Sir Richard Crookes had laid their reputations on the line to claim that life is continuous. We just go through another door, and we progress where we left off in life, in a sort of a gradual spiritual development. I hadn't yet run across the medical studies of Dr. Raymond A. Moody in his book *Life After Life*, or Dr. Elisabeth Kübler-Ross's studies of dying patients. They were also two scientists who put their reputations on the line. I wished I had known about their studies at that time. It would have speeded my own learning process.

It was apparent from the start that Laura and both the Chamberses liked John enough to put up with his persistent use of phrases such as "the alleged apparition," or "That's evidence, but it's not proof," or "That's all well and fine, but is it documented?" or "You mind running that by me once again?" But they could handle him. They gave it right back to him. "Yes, John 'Alleged' Fuller," they would say.

Laura had whipped up some incredible strawberry shortcake, not exactly thinny thin, but in spite of the bulging zipper on my jeans, I indulged myself. While downing it with some English tea, straight from Nassau, Laura told us of her experience in a meditation circle, and her apparent communication with Don Repo. But before she could even finish, John popped in with his usual diplomacy:

"Come on, Laura: do you *really* believe that you were in touch with Repo? How could you possibly expect me or anyone else to believe that?"

Laura had caught on to John. She didn't bat an eye. "Of course I do, I told you last time I saw you that Don Repo wants you to write the story. Don also said that he wants his wife to know."

"I'd have to have more evidence than that—" John didn't finish his statement, but we all got the message.

"John," Laura said. "Don said that his wife

would be receptive to his communications. He is very adamant about wanting this story out, and now that he knows it will be written, he's more at ease."

"Wait a minute, Laura—" Both of John's arms had stretched out into the air, as if he were receiving a pass on the 20-yard line. "I didn't make any commitment. I'm still investigating the possibility that there may be something here."

Laura had come out with some of the damndest statements. She seemed to *assume* belief in communications with the "other side" as a matter of course. John's point was that there had to be clear evidence, not just a medium's subjective impression that she *thought* she was communicating.

Laura was as stubborn as John. "You'll see," she said. "We're not honest-to-God idiots, you know."

Stan broke into the conversation. "What John doesn't know is the background and theory of all this. It takes a lot for someone to learn what we've already proved to ourselves."

I was dangling halfway between John and the others in the conversation. The books I had read had opened me up a little, but I had a long way to go.

John came in with, "Look. This is an intriguing story, and I'm not trying to put a wet blanket on it. All I'm saying is I need a lot more evidence. I'm not a negative skeptic. I'm a benevolent skeptic. If you, Stan, have taken all the trouble to go through this 'soul rescue' idea, it's a persuasive point. But I've got to know more. I'm still not sure if there's a book here."

I knew that wasn't quite the truth. John was leaning heavily toward writing the book, but he was just keeping his usual respectable journalistic distance, as he so often called it.

I was anxious to ask Carol and Stan many of the

questions I hadn't been able to ask Manning. "If Repo really is appearing on the L-1011," I said, "what is he trying to say? Is he trying to communicate?"

"Yes, we believe so, Elizabeth," Carol said. "He's trying to get through to the flight attendants and pilots and tell them what happened. I'm almost convinced of that."

"You mean they don't know how the plane crashed?" I asked. "I thought it was all made clear at the NTSB hearing."

"Yes," Stan replied, "you're half right. It was for the most part made clear, but the pilots took a lot more of the blame than was due them. It was a series of circumstances that led to the crash. It wasn't just the fault of the flight crew."

"So he's coming back because of guilt?" I asked.

"Partly," Stan said. "But I think he also feels very protective of the L-1011. He knows that structurally it's a good plane. We all do in the business. In fact it's probably the best in the air. I get the distinct impression that Don wants to clear the pilots' names and the plane's reputation. Does that make sense?"

"I think so," I said.

"And to do this," Stan continued, "I figure he's used all his energy and strength to manifest himself and get their attention. As if to say, 'Here I am.'"

"But sometimes he seemed to frighten the stews," I said.

"That's why we were concerned for this man," Stan said. "If all the studies in parapsychology are true, he didn't know what state he was in. He had a message, and was trying to get it across. But apparently there was no one he could get it through to."

"So we conducted this soul rescue," Carol said.

John had told me a little bit about the soul rescue but it was still vague in my mind.

I was currently reading a book about Eileen Garrett, one of the most famous of the modern mediums. She talked about her spiritual guide who "came through" when she was in a trance state. At these times, her voice deepened and her whole aspect changed. Although she claimed to be in awe of her guide, she was not aware of how or why he had come to her. She even believed that this guide may have been a split-off of her own personality. Mrs. Garrett had been tested by Dr. Adolph Meyer, a noted psychologist and psychiatrist at Johns Hopkins University. His final analysis was that her mind had developed another channel, and that channel had to be filled somehow. I asked Carol and Stan if they used a guide for their soul rescue.

"Yes," Carol said. "Our guides helped to bring Don through. We saw him physically, and he showed us exactly what had transpired down in the hell hole."

"Hold everything Carol," John interrupted. "What do you mean, you 'saw him physically'? You mean like I see all of you here?"

Carol smiled back at John, almost as if she were waiting for his comments. "We saw him through thought impressions. Is that better, John?"

"Sort of. Thank you." John leaned back in the canvas chair. He seemed unconvinced.

Carol continued, "He also showed us what his thoughts were when the crash took place. His extreme frustration. He seemed to indicate that he loved his wife, and wanted to be here with her."

"He appeared to love her very much," Stan added. "It was as if this was the first time he could get these feelings out and talk about them."

"What do you mean, 'talk.' Did you hear him vocally say something?" John asked.

"No he communicated it to us, again through thought impressions," Stan answered.

I'm sure John had a rough idea of what Stan meant, but he always likes people to clarify everything. It was one of his little hang-ups. Laura finally told John he had a tendency to get boring after a while, but he just ignored her.

Stan continued, "So we've tried to help Don realize that he was no longer on the earth level."

"And that he has graduated to a better life," Laura added.

"You mean like he left kindergarten?" I said.

"Well," Carol said, "that's one way of putting it."

I still wasn't so sure of the difference between a soul rescue and an exorcism. I asked them if they would mind explaining it.

"There's a big difference," Stan said. "An exorcism is to get rid of a negative entity or influence. The soul rescue is when you help someone make a transition from a physical reality to a spirit reality. But due to one cause or another, the spirit is still earthbound."

"The spiritual self still thinks he is in the physical realm," Carol added. "He won't face the fact that he's a spirit."

"Was that the case with Don?" I asked.

"We think so," Stan said. "He apparently became confused in this state. See, the sudden transition of the spirit can create a state of turmoil. Often this results from a sudden death. You try to get them to realize they are no longer in body, but in spirit. That's the first step."

That was almost the same explanation that Dick Manning gave for his deliverance, I thought.

"You get them to open up their eyes to see the light," Carol said. "It's like you're looking through a big long tunnel, and you see a little spot of light at the other end. And it's pitch black up to that point, but there are people or conductors and it is their job to take the new spirit and guide him up this corridor into the light." At this moment, I was really having a hard time visualizing all this. But later, I was to find out that this was completely in line with Dr. Moody's and Dr. Kübler-Ross's medical studies.

"That's right," Laura added. "Once they get into this light, then they can start expanding. Then, if they want, they can come back to communicate with those still in the physical realm."

"There's lots of factors involved in a soul rescue," Stan said. "It may be that a person who has passed over had very strong convictions before he died, and he goes over with those same strong convictions. He may believe that he's going to some sort of a purgatory, and may not want to accept the light at first."

"Was Don Repo supposed to be a physical, solid being in these appearances?" John asked.

"We believe so," Stan replied. "It takes a tremendous amount of energy to manifest the way he did."

This was the hang-up I had, and I was sure John had it too. How could some sort of solid being simply appear or reappear in front of crew members? Even after reading the British reports, I had trouble with this.

Stan continued: "Normally the reason they appear as in a fog is that the intensity of the person's energy is low. The more intense the thought-image—the more intense the energy will be, which will ultimately cause a more detailed physical image. Repo must have had a very intense energy pattern."

"Does that mean that since the soul rescue and deliverance that Don Repo won't be appearing anymore on the L-1011s?" I asked.

"Well, it's been over a year since the soul rescue," Stan said. "And we haven't heard any reports of his reappearing."

"He seems to have moved into the Light," Carol added. "Although he still might have a concern for both the airplane and his family."

"When you pass into spirit there's evidence that your family is very important to you," Laura said.

In *Survival of Death*, a book I was studying then, Paul Beard stated that it was important to learn as much as possible about ESP between the living. Otherwise, it would be easy to attribute to telepathy from the dead what may really be telepathy from the living. I couldn't help but think that maybe this was the case with Laura and the Chamberses' communications. But I would not make a judgment, at least not until we left Laura's apartment.

"One of Repo's first words during my last meditation circle," Laura continued, "was that he will be with you, John, and he will continue to help you on the research for the book."

"Knock it off, Laura," John said. He meant it, too.

"*Really*, John," she said. "He knows that you're the right one to do the book, and that you'll do it properly."

"Laura."

"Okay, okay, you'll see."

"Laura," John kept repeating. "I can take just so much."

"See, John," Stan said, smiling. "Don could theoretically spot you as a good channel."

"Come on," John said. "What was in that strawberry shortcake?"

"Why do you keep resisting this story?" Laura asked.

"Because I'm thinking about what my editor is going to say. He already thinks I clap for Tinker Bell." I was beginning to think that I might become guilty of the same thing.

John dropped me at my hotel. He had to come in to New York from Connecticut the next day, and he suggested we meet for lunch. My flight didn't leave La Guardia until early evening, so I could make it. We could discuss Laura, the Chamberses, and our next move in one package.

At noon on the dot, John's white Audi pulled up in front of the hotel. I was keeping a lookout so that he wouldn't have to park. I watched from behind the glass entrance doors as he leaped out of the driver's seat, walked over to the passenger's side, and began heaving what looked like an entire secondhand bookstore into the back seat. The car was definitely a place where old books went to die. In spite of his efforts to clear the deck, I still had to maneuver my 5'3" frame into the front seat.

John knew of a charming little Japanese restaurant in the East Fifties. There were only two tables per cubbyhole, sectioned off with rice-paper screens. The tables sat on a slightly raised platform, covered with straw mats. We were instructed to take off our shoes. After we plopped down on the straw mats, we both stuffed our legs under the squatty table.

Before we got into a heavy discussion of the night

before, we ordered drinks and lunch. John made a point of asking the kimono-clad waitress if she would mind getting rid of the sticks, and bringing him a fork and knife. He told me that if God meant for man to use chopsticks, we would have been born with bamboo fingernails.

I was rather proud of my digital dexterity with chopsticks. For the last three years, I had been flying Tokyo layovers. Due to a skimpy meal allowance, crew members used to frequent the more out-of-the-way restaurants where a knife and fork were something out of an American Western flick. After the meal was prepared in front of us and the tea was poured, we began discussing the previous night's adventures.

"John, you were really pretty rough with Laura," I said. He had not only questioned her beliefs, he had questioned her sanity as well. If I were Laura, I would have flattened him.

"Maybe," he said. "But I had to be rough."

"How come?" I asked.

"Because Laura just can't assume that everybody believes what she believes."

"You believe that Don Repo has been telling them that he wants you to write the story?"

"You kidding?" he asked.

"No. I'm very serious. Some of the books I've been reading say it could be possible. Not that I believe everything I read." I was also thinking about my experience at the séance. For some unexplainable reason, I felt as if those names had to have come from someplace other than my conscious or subconscious mind. I was also thinking about the stories of the other people we had met. There were too many factors which seemed to be building toward the incredible.

"There seems to be a medium everywhere we look," John said.

"I know," I said. "It's hard to believe."

John said, "The problem is, I can't afford not to thoroughly investigate these stories, now that I've gone this far. If they don't check out, that means the book doesn't check out. Sometimes I feel like dropping the whole damn thing."

"I know that," I said. "But you won't."

"How do you know I won't?" he asked.

"Because this whole thing intrigues you too much—you're hooked," I said.

"I might be hooked, but I'm not going to be taken in," he said. "You see, all these stories hinge on just one thing."

"What's that?"

"The validity of the people you interview," he said. "You can go to Bellevue and get some of the greatest stories ever told."

"You're not trying to say that all these people we've been interviewing are nuts—are you?" I asked.

"That's what I can't figure out. All of them seem as normal as pizza pie, except for one thing," he said.

"What's that?"

"This wild, unbelievable ghost story."

"Wait a minute. What about my experience in the Miami séance?" I was still puzzled about that.

John laughed. "How can I be sure about someone who falls asleep in an overhead rack?"

"Very funny," I said. "I should have known better than to tell you that story."

"That story is one of the things that make me feel you're non-psychic," he said. "Which is a welcome contrast these days."

"I may not be psychic, but that séance freaked me out. Still does."

"That's another one of the things I wanted to talk to you about today," he said.

"The overhead rack?"

"No, your experience at the Miami séance."

"What about it?" I asked. "Did you believe it?"

"I believe it enough to try some more experiments," he said. This was a new tack. I didn't quite expect John to be so willing to dig into something like this.

"Are you thinking of another séance?" I asked.

"More than that," he said. "The last time I was in Florida, somebody mentioned something about a school called the Arthur Ford Academy. It's sort of allied with the Spiritual Frontiers group. In fact, Patricia and Bud Hayes run it."

"A whole school in parapsychology?" I asked.

"That's what that fellow J.R. Worden claims. In fact, he's studied there. Anyway J.R. was talking to Patricia after your séance and she said she'd like to see you again. You impressed her with the information that came through you that evening," John said.

"You serious?" I asked.

"I am. That's exactly what J.R. said, anyway."

"Impressed with me?"

"Pat seemed to think that you were a natural channel," John said.

"A what?"

"J.R. explained that we're all psychic. I guess to some degree, anyway. Except some of us are supposed to be more than others. According to Patricia, you may be a medium waiting to happen."

"I really never had any kind of psychic experience before," I pointed out.

"I'm going back down next week to finish up the oceanographic film," John said. "I'll go over to the Academy with J.R. and check it out."

"I really liked the Hayeses," I said. "In fact, I was supposed to get back to Patricia after the séance. But I never did."

"Just as well," John said. "It's better not to jump into anything."

"Okay, but I'm really interested in following this up—I mean if the school is legit and all that."

"Let's wait and see," he said. Then he added: "This could be good, deep background research, anyway."

One of the books I had been reading said something about how an investigation could be more than just an inquiry. It could also become an experience. From the start this whole research project had been an experience, one that was headed in my direction, whether I was ready for it or not.

After John paid the bill, he mentioned he had to stop a few blocks away. He asked if I wanted to go along. He said that I wouldn't be bored.

"Where is it, another séance?" I asked.

"Nothing like that," he said.

"Maxwell's Plum?" I asked.

"You know I hate rock music and crowded joints."

"Where, then?"

"Not far. I just have to drop off some papers to Uri Geller at his apartment.

"I didn't know that you knew Geller?" I said.

"I just finished an article on him for *The Reader's Digest*."

I was surprised he hadn't mentioned Uri Geller before. Especially since we had been discussing so many aspects of the paranormal. Uri was known everywhere as the Israeli psychic who was able to bend metal by the power of his mind. However, he was highly controversial.

"Is that guy for real?" I asked.

John never liked to answer questions directly. He just began naming places where Geller had been tested. Places such as Stanford Research Institute, Max Planck Institute of Plasma Physics, Birkbeck College of the University of London—the names were all very impressive.

"But what's your opinion?" I asked.

"Uri convinced the editors and researchers at *The Reader's Digest*," John said. "I know magic tricks, and I know what he does is definitely not what the magicians do." Changing gears, he asked, "Have you got a key with you?"

I did. I always had my cockpit key with me—part of in-flight equipment.

"Good," John said. Then he became reflective. "There's so little we all really know. It bugs me."

At that point I began to realize that there was very little I knew about John. I knew he had been divorced for the past eight years. He had two grown boys, and one still growing. He hated rock music almost as much as he hated eggplant.

I was really curious as to why he hadn't mentioned Geller to me before. There had been plenty of opportunities. Unless, of course, he thought Geller was just a phony. But he didn't appear to think that. John had another flaw. He would never commit himself to anything. Every time he got into a sticky situation, he immediately began to quote everybody from Emerson to P.T. Barnum. I was always amazed at all the information he had filed away underneath that Abercrombie's fishing hat.

Uri Geller's East Side apartment was also his office. The walls were plastered with articles, book jackets, photos of him in action, and his own art work.

Geller was just too good-looking. He had the most magnetic pair of eyes I've ever seen in one face. If you like good-looking men, you'd flip for him. Luckily, I don't. I like those who have sort of a seedy look about them. And who are basically insecure. But on top of having looks, Geller was pleasingly disarming.

Sitting in the living room–office were Uri, Shippi, his business manager, and Trina and Frida, his two secretaries. John told me later that Uri considers them all like his family. Whenever he travels, the entourage travels.

I was wearing my airline uniform since John was planning to drive me back to the airport on his way to Westport. I went to extensive lengths to make sure that my cockpit key was always on my person. I prided myself that in nearly seven years I had never lost or forgotten it. Without this small key, a flight attendant doesn't get into the cockpit. Due to security, the door must be locked at all times. And there's another tacit rule, not in our manual: You don't bug the guys in the cockpit to open the door from the inside.

The reason I never lost my key was an ingenious device I had invented. I had the key on a chain, and the chain was sewn on my skirt. Permanently. Even when I had it dry-cleaned, it stayed on.

And that would also be part of the problem. Not my problem, but Geller's problem. According to some magicians, one of the ways Geller bent metal was not by the power of his mind, but by substituting keys. But now I could play 007 and uncover the truth. There was no way my key was coming off my uniform, unless the whole skirt went with it. And that I might notice. I couldn't wait for the appropriate time to ask Geller if he could bend my key.

But I didn't have to. He noticed it first.

"What a strange place to keep a key," he said as he lifted it out from my skirt. "Do you always keep it there?"

I laughed and explained why. As I did, I looked down at the key. He was no longer touching it. But you've got to believe me, it was curling up, and I mean *curling*. I watched in horror. The bending was very slow, but there was no question about it. It continued to bend after he had walked away.

I was astonished. I sat back down on the large sofa. If this were true, Geller belonged somewhere between Houdini and the Pyramids. But then I thought back to the time my uncle made smoke come out of his ears. I used to herd packs of kids into the house to watch my uncle smoke. But, I thought, I was fooled once. This could just be a more sophisticated trick. I would have to think this one over.

Geller had left the room. For some reason, I began to check my jewelry to make sure it hadn't dematerialized. My gold ring was still intact. So was my gold bracelet. Around my neck was the 18-karat gold cross I always wore. But the cross was out of sight under my blouse, and my blouse was securely buttoned all the way up. Over that was my scarf—part of my official uniform. The scarf was secured to my blouse by the Northwest gold logo pin. And over all of that was my blazer. There was no way Geller could have known about that gold cross, unless he had X-ray vision. I even wondered about that.

For some reason I reached down and plucked the cross out and looked at it. I then saw the ninth wonder of the world. Right in front of my eyes, the cross was bending. For seconds, I was speechless. Then I yelled for Geller to come back into the room, and stop it from snapping in two. After several more seconds, it came to rest at a 45-degree angle.

Everybody was still in the room, except Geller. Everybody saw what had happened, but nobody acted like it was any big deal. John then leaned over and said, "Don't worry. I don't know how the hell he does it, either. I would have told you about it, if I'd thought you'd believe me."

I saw it happen. Geller was nowhere near me. He wasn't even in the room. If he had tried to get at the cross, my matronly dignity would have forced me to deck him.

I couldn't wait to get back to the airport, and show off my bent key. It *had* happened. It *was* incredible. It would be a great conversation piece. A total party-stopper.

I was the hit of the flight back to MSP. The other two stewardesses were telling the passengers the story about the key. After we landed and I was saying goodbye to the people, more than half wanted to have a look at the bent hunk of metal. They ignored the open cockpit door. Usually passengers peek their heads in, and nod in the captain's direction. But nobody did. I think the captain's dignity was a little bruised by this. We all reassured him that a bent key was no competition for a 727 captain. We lied.

When I arrived back at the scheduling building, I signed in, as you do after every flight. You still have to be in full uniform. Of course, allowances are made. For instance, if you sign in wearing a lasagna dinner—you merely blame it on clear air turbulence. Or bumpy air, as they prefer you to call it. The word turbulence is a no-no. Something in our manual says that it scares people. Personally I always thought it would scare passengers more to hear the crew use baby talk. Especially, the captain.

Anyway as I signed my name in the big loose-leaf notebook, I asked the person propped up behind the desk if I might have another cockpit key. She said the obvious: "What happened to yours?" I showed her the deformed key dangling on my skirt, and she just simply handed me a new one. She didn't even blink. Just like that. I didn't like that, I wanted to share my incredible experience.

So I asked her, "Aren't you going to ask me what happened?"

She said, "Okay, what happened? You dropped it in the biffy."

I was offended. "Not at all," I said. "You've heard of this guy, Uri Geller? He just touched it, and it bent. It kept on bending after he stopped. Can you believe it?"

She said, "Oh." Just like that. "Oh." That was all.

Then she called over her shoulder to the next office. "Hey, Leda. You wanna come out here and hear *this* one?"

When Leda came out, the supervisor said, "Elizabeth, would you mind repeating that?"

I did.

And then Leda called over her shoulder. "Hey. Dorothy, Ginny, come on out and get a load of this."

So I repeated the story again, probably with a

little more enthusiasm because of all the attention it was getting. Then, all of a sudden, they just walked away. And that was it. I could tell now that I was dealing with confined horizons.

I had four days off between trips. I was glad. I needed that time to read and reflect. I found myself being catapulted into a strange, new world. A world that was not closed in by conventional horizons.

In a short time span, I had been confronted for the first time in my life with such phenomena as UFOs, ghosts, séances, exorcisms, and Geller. I was also confronted with one gigantic paradox—Fuller. He was so cautious, so afraid of being taken for a sucker. But at the same time, he had a passion for exploration into the unknown. John was actually my healthy balance between the two extremes. He tempered the heavy scenes with a sense of humor. During interviews he seemed oblivious to the fact that he had a great wit. That's probably what made his directness so tolerable.

My first impulse was to justify these stories as merely subjective accounts. But the evidence with every interview was mounting in measurable proportions. I had to keep reminding myself that it would be just as unfair to be overly critical and skeptical as it would to be overly accepting and gullible.

In reading Kenneth Richmond's *Evidence of Reality*, I came across an interesting theory. According to Richmond, Manning, the Chamberses, Laura, and Ginny Packard had had purely subjective experiences; like a religious experience, theirs had reality primarily for them. Their experiences were *not* common property. But Betty Hill had seen the UFO along with her husband, Barney.

73

Elizabeth Fuller

No longer was her experience purely subjective. My recent experience with Geller probably belonged to what Richmond said was common property. The bending of my key and my cross, was observed by others in addition to myself.

My own experience in the Miami séance does not qualify either as subjective or common property. It was not really totally subjective. I had never before laid eyes on the man sitting next to me, yet he kept getting answers to what I was saying. And the answers all checked out.

I suppose it could be argued that he was using telepathy. But then again, nobody in the circle, including me, knew any of the passengers. There's another factor that could be argued: I could have seen those names in the newspaper three years ago, filed them away in my mental computer, and dug them up for the occasion. But that theory is almost as far out as spirit communications.

After carefully analyzing all of these situations, and spending hour after hour reflecting and reading different theories, I came to my own brilliant conclusion: Something is going on out there, and I was bound and determined to find out what. But what I didn't know was that this growing curiosity was going to lead me far beyond my original 007 assignment.

Chapter V

I WAS LIVING a double life. Roughly fourteen days a month, I followed the Northwest Airlines Operations Manual semi-scrupulously. One section has to do with the way you look. I had to reflect credibility upon the company, was the way they put it. My uniform would always have to be neat, clean, brushed, pressed, and in good repair.

That was only the beginning. My legs had to be kept free of hair, and the gold logo pin had to be centered over the thread marker on the front of my hat. I could only wear a hairstyle if it was approved by a supervisor. But then only if it was secured at the nape of the neck with a grosgrain ribbon, black in winter and white in summer, exactly one inch in width. The hair could be no longer than eight inches below the ribbon. All two thousand of us were computerized to look like the Northwest Orient brochure.

These pontifical rules made me think back to when I was block president for the Mickey Mouse Club. I held a meeting every Saturday morning immediately following *Rin-Tin-Tin*. Since I was president, I laid down the rules. One of the rules was that no kid could show up in the garage without the Mickey Mouse ears and shirt on. Unfortunately, the club folded, as many nonprofit organizations do.

I did manage to maintain my individuality, and I continued to express that in little ways. Like wearing my oversized hoop earrings, and pitching that tacky one-inch grosgrain to let my hair flow free. Also, I substituted modified platform shoes for those orthopedic Boy Scout walkers. However, by defying the "bible," you're taking a chance. If you get caught as a nonconformist, you automatically receive a small pink slip in your company mailbox. That pink slip means you have not been atta-girl, and if you receive two more, you're grounded like an oil-soaked penguin.

The company tries to make sure you don't violate the manual. One way they do this is by putting an airline snoop on the payroll. Of course this is not really that unusual; most airlines and many department stores and other businesses have spies. But I think ours had the only snoop who took her training directly from the Watergate Plumbers. Even if we all didn't know what she looked like on occasion, no paying passenger would carry an old *Life* magazine that flips open into a dog-eared notebook!

The snoop's job is to fly around on the airplane and bug the cabin attendants in every possible way. For instance, if you're coming down the aisle with five trays in your arms and a plastic glass under your chin, she'll stop you and ask you to immediately adjust her air vent.

Any cabin attendant's first reaction would be to kill. But in airline training school, you learn not to respond to your first reactions. Your second reaction is to ask her politely if she would mind waiting until you drop the trays off in the galley. You then bite your tongue, and reassure her that you will *promptly* return. Any normal passenger would understand, except the company snoop is programmed to give the attendant a hard time.

Fortunately, most cabin attendants could handle her. We simply addressed her by name. She hated that more than begonias. She would deny her name to the bitter end. But at least she got the message that we were on to her. And in most cases, she would drop the undercover-agent bit.

Our company snoop never made the international flights. And I was glad of that. I was currently on my way from Honolulu to Tokyo, all 365 passengers were tucked in. The movie, a "Bambi Goes to Hawaii"-type production, was over. I had six hours left to do nothing. I was too bogged down with jet lag even to read some of the books on parapsychology I had with me. I couldn't take the chance of falling asleep again while on duty. I could probably talk to the other cabin attendants, but after the first two days you run out of things to talk about. So you can either kill time by pouring huge 12-cup carriers of Coke and 7-Up, or you can wake up an interesting looking passenger and offer him a junior set of wings. I chose to do none of the above.

I sat down on my jump seat with a mug of hot, black coffee to keep awake. My thoughts wandered back to my last meeting with John.

On our drive from Geller's apartment to the airport, we talked about Uri's strange powers, and how he seems to violate all the laws of physics and conventional science. We also talked about other people who experience such things as clairvoyance, telepathy, and out-of-body phenomena. John felt it was extremely important to eliminate the strong prejudices against the study and development of our knowledge of the paranormal. On the other hand, he felt nothing could be taken for granted, and that you needed twice the caution when working in an area like this. That was why John was so careful about his research. He wanted to be certain that he was doing a serious investigation into this ghost story—not just a sensationalized spook book.

When we arrived at La Guardia, I discovered that my flight was delayed two hours due to a mechanical problem. John insisted on waiting out the delay with me. I sat down in a tiny booth in the coffee shop. John went to the self-service counter for coffee, and brought back two huge hunks of cheesecake to go with it. I hated myself for eating it, but I justified the caloric intake by using Sweet n' Low rather than sugar in my coffee.

For the first time in the course of the research, John and I didn't discuss our project. That was a welcome relief. Too much had happened in the previous twenty-four hours. I had reached my psychic saturation point.

Although I had told John about my divorce, I never went any further than a passing mention. But for some reason, we got around to talking about it. I told him that I couldn't shake the guilty feeling. He said that he could identify with what I was going through because of his divorce. I felt embarrassed and dropped the subject. I knew John had sensed my guarded feelings and he quickly switched to the blessings and hassles of travel. It was another subject we both could relate to.

John began telling me about his recent research in Africa, where he had been chasing a killer virus through the Nigerian highlands. Its first victim had been a nurse in a lonely mission hospital. To find the carrier or host, virologists began working around the clock in their germ-proof labs. Two virologists in the Yale University labs were stricken simply by examining the blood serum. When one died, the research stopped. They had to incinerate all but one batch of the blood specimens at Yale. The remaining specimen was then transferred to the federal maximum-security labs in Atlanta, Georgia— something straight out of *The Andromeda Strain*.

Meanwhile, the disease was rampant in Africa. Thousands of people faced death unless a cure was found. During the search for the insidious killer, John was living in mission huts and eating mission food, rats included.

Shortly after he had eaten rat meat, the scientists discovered that the virus came from a certain type of rat in the Nigerian Sudan. After eating the potentially deadly meat, John came down with all the symptoms of lassa fever: sore throat, high temperature, headache, and nausea. As a devout hypochondriac, he was convinced that he had ten days. Scared for his life, he went to the doctor at the mission hospital, the same hospital that had housed the first victim of lassa fever. The doctor examined him thoroughly and came up with an instant prognosis: he would live. He had a touch of the flu. John refused to believe the doctor. He counted off each day he had left. For the first time since he had arrived at the lonely mission, he swapped his two carefully rationed Dewar's scotches a day for a prayer meeting—just in case. But ten days passed, and John lived to tell the story.

Across the table, John described to me what it was like going to sleep with a net screen wrapped snugly around his bed and a club by his side, just in case of a late-night visit from a rat or viper. He described rat meat as a sickish sweet version of white chicken meat. And he began to describe camel's milk but he couldn't quite find anything to compare it with. I didn't press him. Here, I thought, was either Dr. Livingston or a guy with a serious death wish.

Our topic switched from the bush to the galley. We exchanged quick recipes for cooking for one. John was proud of being able to whip together a three-course dinner, simply by placing three unopened cans of food, such as peas, corned beef hash, and boiled potatoes into a pot of boiling water. Then you just waited ten minutes and pinched them out with a pair of pliers. He claimed it was total efficiency. No pans to clean. My recipes operated on a similar principle. I could whip up anything from a Stouffer's dinner-in-a-pouch to frozen Quiche Lorraine, then pitch the wrapper and pretend I had slaved over a hot stove.

John asked if I did anything on my days off, other than read parapsychology books and cook exotic meals. I told him that my life was really pretty humdrum, contrary to what people imagine the life of a stewardess to be like. He looked surprised. He said he bet that half of Minneapolis was pounding at my door. I told him that I had actually only been out a couple of times, and then it hadn't been really a date type of thing. I had more or less been filling up a foursome.

For some reason, I don't think he believed me. I went on to explain about the hang-ups Catholic school had left me with and that, ridiculous as it sounded, I was sort of in a state of mourning. I still don't think he believed me. But he did say that that was probably good, he didn't want to lose his ace investigator to some guy, especially in the middle of the research.

I told John that I'd ask him about his life when he wasn't so busy. I already had my preconceived ideas. He asked me what they were. So I told him that I imagined him to live in a small shack with papers and books strewn everywhere and, maybe, a few cobwebs. He wanted to know how I knew what his house looked like. He then went on to tell me about a friend of his. Before he would come over to visit John, he claimed he had to get a typhoid shot. He was kidding—I think ...

A call button went off in the dark 747. It quickly brought me back from Africa and rats, a tiny shack, and gourmet cooking, to somewhere near the International Date Line. As I was attending to a thirsty passenger, it hit me. Why had John said: "I don't want to lose my ace investigator to some guy, especially in the middle of the research." Could he have been jealous? Then I remembered the time John had phoned and my roommate's friend had answered the phone. John wanted to know who he was. I just assumed he wanted to know because of journalistic instinct. But now I was wondering if it could have been more than that. I never thought of myself as romantically involved with John. I didn't even know how old he was, but from what I gathered, he had two sons around my age. No. The idea of an involvement was probably just my imagination.

For the next seven days, I pored over Paul Beard's book, *Survival of Death*. It became sort of my psychic guidebook. I was looking for possible alternatives to Laura Britebarth's and the Chamberses' communications. Many of my doubts lay in the fact that I hadn't experienced what they had. Even though I believed in their total sincerity, that just wasn't enough. I wanted to remain objective and the only way to do that was to go with the facts.

And there were no *real* facts. All of their purported messages were purely subjective. It was only possible to listen to their comments. I was frustrated. I wanted to observe how they came by the communications, but I couldn't, I was simply not a medium. I could not hear or see what they claimed to hear and see.

Beard's book discussed the extreme importance of being cautious, but he also acknowledged the other extreme, the total skeptic. The negative skeptic does not produce any sort of an explanation to show that the medium was not in touch with the spirit world. He just claims that it was impossible for a medium to get information from that sphere. Psychic research should consider the negative point of view as unacceptable, unless supported by as much evidence as was required of a positive point of view. A line had to be drawn between productive skepticism and an attitude which prevented any positive theory from ever being offered. Only then, Beard claims, can there be a healthy trend in psychic research.

The more I read, the more I realized that if this ghost story were true, it would indicate that this isn't our last stop. It might even send me back to church. But if the story weren't true, and John wrote it as if it were factual, then it might set back psychic research fifty years. I knew that neither John nor I wanted to deceive ourselves, or anybody else.

I was so exhausted when I got off that eleven-day Tokyo trip, I didn't even check the mail. It wasn't until the next morning that I noticed John's letter on top of my dresser, along with an envelope stuffed with redeemable coupons addressed: To Occupant. I opened John's letter first.

Dear Liz,

I've been trying to reach you by phone, but forgot you were going on a long 11-day stretch on the Tokyo run. This should reach you when you get back, and put you up to date.

I'm still wavering back and forth on the story. I can't help blowing hot and cold on it. I've adopted Mark Twain's slogan: "Interesting if true, and interesting anyway."

I'm still approaching it on the level that it's a jet-age ghost story, a legend, a myth—and the story would be just how something like this could grow in the modern age. If we don't go beyond that, it would be interesting.

But these other things keep coming up that point to a much more serious inquiry. There's the life-after-death theme. When you get right down to it, this is just about the most important question that we can examine. It would be nice to be a theological conformist, and just accept what the Church says about it. But their hard-nail evidence is very weak, and you have to accept everything on faith.

I've been interviewing several Eastern crew members, and some of them claim direct, firsthand encounters. Will give you details later. Others have collected and catalogued incidents very methodically. I've talked to the FAA man from Atlanta who is a medium, and he was impressive. I've got another appointment with him, and on your next trip I hope you can meet him and give me your opinion. Also, the other crew members I've talked to. They include, incidentally, a mechanic who observed the shop crew removing the nonstructural parts from the plane where most of the apparitions have allegedly occurred. People are still reluctant to talk. The idea of being sent to the company shrink if they report anything like this, is not attractive. If any of this is true, Repo seems to be a very gentle and helpful apparition, and all the pilots like the L-1011, so it's not a dismal story. It might even be a helpful one.

I've also talked to J.R. and Patricia and Bud Hayes about the courses at the Arthur Ford Academy. From what I gather, it's sort of like these courses all over the country on Mind Control, or consciousness expansion. The difference seems to be the loose connection with the Spiritual Frontiers Fellowship, in that they include the spiritual side.

Anyway, Patricia suggested that you take the three-day crash course in psychic sensitivity, focusing on mediumship. It's something like fourteen hours a day, very intensive. J.R. took it, and says he got a lot out of it. The Hayeses said that this particular course is for those who already show a marked degree of psychic sensitivity. They seem to think that you would fit into that category. I didn't tell them about the overhead rack. . . .

Since it's all part of the background research, I think the course is worth a try if you are agreeable. There's one coming up in two weeks, if you can take the time off. It will be paid for as part of the research.

I'm about as psychically sensitive as a cow, so it wouldn't do any good for me to take it. But Patricia said it would be okay for me to audit the class, as a journalistic onlooker. After your experience in that séance, who knows what might happen. See if you can read up on Arthur Ford, a very famous medium who was responsible for the founding of the Academy under his own name.

Let me know as soon as you can, and best of luck.

> Faithfully,
> Benedict Arnold

I hadn't been expecting another letter from John. Especially one that indicated I might have some psychic ability. I had never before thought of myself as having anything in addition to the usual five senses. And I still didn't—even after the Miami séance. I was sure that was a one-time shot. It would never happen again. I was no threat to the Maharishi Mahesh Yogi.

I must admit the idea of taking the course was tempting. But on the other hand, I didn't want to build up any false expectations for John, expectations that I knew I wouldn't be able to live up to. In fact, I didn't really think the school would actually check out. John was always so cautious. I felt certain that he would phone and tell me that the place wasn't legit. The whole idea was so weird—a course in mediumship. I was wondering what the final exam would be—multiple choice on the Ouija board?

I was both excited about the prospect and scared. Not scared that the goblins were going to get me, as much as: what if there really is something out there? I didn't want my life to change. I wasn't searching for any extras. I mean, it was cool for me to investigate the paranormal, but I wasn't so sure I wanted to be part of it. I thought it over before I wrote John back:

Dear Benedict Arnold:

For the last three days, I've been trying to phone you with no luck. Your answering service seemed to think that you were floating around somewhere south of the Mason-Dixon Line. But they assured me that you would get my message.

Just in case your editor had you committed to a rubber room, I decided to drop you a line. In spite of what the Hayeses think, I doubt if I have any marked degree of psychic ability. I know the séance was strange, but that was only one time out of twenty-eight years. I've been reading a lot lately about mediums, and most of them claim to have been psychic since the womb. I'm not telling you this to discourage you—I'm just giving you fair warning.

You also mentioned that the course is sort of similar to TM, or Mind Control. Again, I don't want to be discouraging, but I've tried meditation, and failed. For two weeks I set aside the twenty minutes in the morning and evening. I followed the "simple breathing technique"—and nothing. I fell asleep after about seven and a half minutes. The book claimed that meditating was as easy and natural as breathing. But I didn't need a book to learn how to breathe. I even considered taking the three-day TM course, but I couldn't see how getting a secret "mantra" would help me to stay awake.

I'm telling you this so you can consider my psychic potential, and then decide for yourself. Anyway, if you do want to go ahead with "Spook U.," I found someone who will trip-trade with me. That would give me seven days off in a row. Time enough to take the course and even go visit the FAA guy in Atlanta.

Which reminds me, we had an FAA guy on one of our legs, San Francisco to Honolulu. I went up to the cockpit and casually asked the crew what they knew about the Eastern ghost. The captain knew a few of the stories, but didn't elaborate, mainly because the FAA guy was breathing down his back. This inspector kept looking at me the entire time, as if I had been nipping away in the galley. It really blows my mind that you found an FAA guy who is a medium. I will have to see that one.

I didn't get any new earth-shattering ghost stories. But while I was laying over in Hawaii, I had lunch with a close friend, who used to fly for Aloha Airlines. She not only knew of the Eastern ghost—she also knew the name Repo. Can you believe that—this ghost story has got legs.

You can call me anytime up until Thursday. After Thursday, I'll be on a short, three-day trip. Then from Monday on, I'll be around.... See you later.

> Yours unflaggingly,
> Betsy Ross

P.S. I'm still freaked out over Geller. I keep my bent cockpit key on my skirt—right next to the new one. Every time I start thinking about this crazy ghost story, I look at the key.

Even though I hadn't heard from John until I returned from my three-day trip, I felt certain that he would want me to take the course at the Academy. And I was right. Monday morning I received a short note from him, followed up by a phone call that same evening:

Dear Betsy Ross:
    Don't worry about being a star psychic— the course is for background research only, and it might even be a big waste of time. I'll ring you Monday, sometime early evening.

> Cryptically,
> King Tut

That evening after John phoned, I picked up a book on Arthur Ford. I had taken it out of the library the date I received John's letter, but I hadn't had a chance to read it. I knew absolutely nothing about Arthur Ford, except that Patricia and Bud Hayes ran the Academy named after him.

In my reading, I learned that he was one of the world's best-known platform mediums. I also learned that he had been a latent psychic. It wasn't until he was in the First World War that he had his first psychic experience. He dreamed of seeing a casualty list. The men on the list had died from an influenza epidemic. The next day a list was posted. The same names that he had dreamed about were on the list. They were even in the same order. I thought quickly back over my experience at the Miami séance. It was almost identical.

His dreams continued, and each time they would come true. Confused and bewildered, he wrote to his strict, Baptist mother, and asked her if there was any record of insanity in the family. She wrote him back and told him that he had an unbalanced aunt who was a medium. She didn't exactly help matters any.

Several years later he began developing his psychic powers under a guru named Swami Yogandanda. It was at some point during this period that a spiritual guide, named Fletcher, came through while he was in a trance. This guide purported to be a person who at one time lived on earth, and was now in another state of consciousness—though still able to communicate with living people, through the use of Arthur's vocal cords.

Once, Arthur was attending a lecture given by Sir Arthur Conan Doyle, the famous spiritualist and creator of Sherlock Holmes. Doyle invited Ford to join him on the platform. He asked Ford to give a demonstration of his psychic abilities. Afterward, in a newspaper interview, Doyle told reporters that Ford's demonstration was one of the most amazing things he had seen in his forty-one years of psychic exploration.

Ford's record was imposing. His work with the Bishop Pike case brought him world fame. The idea of learning about the psychic in his own house was intriguing. I had actually been startled to discover that my first psychic experience in the séance was similar to his. I was sure that that was where the similarities would end. But I still looked forward to learning more, for better or for worse, in our search for the Ghost of Flight 401.

Chapter VI

I ARRIVED AT Miami International Airport on Thursday evening, as planned. Friday morning would be the first day of the intensive course. As I was collecting my garment bag from one of the cramped 727 closets I thought back to the last time I had been in Miami, the time when I had mysteriously received those names. Stepping out onto the jetway, I could feel the hot, musty Florida air. It suddenly made me realize I had made a commitment. There was no turning back. Tomorrow morning I would be sitting in some sort of classroom at Spook U. I had absolutely no idea what to expect.

I was hoping that I had brought the right clothes. Patricia told John that we should dress comfortably. I didn't think it would be appropriate to ask if black clothes were preferred. I brought jeans and tee shirts. I couldn't even begin to imagine what goes on in a mediumship course. Maybe there would be some sort of repeat performance of that first séance. I wasn't anxious for any surprises. Had I given this course a lot of thought, I would probably still be in Minneapolis. It was too late now.

John was waiting in the gate area with a *New York Times* tucked under his arm. As soon as I got close enough, his long arm snaked over from behind the gate and grabbed my flight bag. He looked as if he had been spending more time on location for the oceanographic film than at his typewriter. He was about ten shades darker than the last time I saw him. He was wearing the summer version of his winter outfit, which was basically the same thing, except sawed off at the knees.

All the way to the Avis Pinto, John and I were chatting as if we had too much to say and not enough time to say it in. We were actually just rehashing our phone conversation of twelve hours earlier.

Before John delivered me to Arthur Ford's former home, we stopped at the New England Oyster House for a large platter of butterfly shrimp. Over dinner, we talked about what we were learning in this strange field. Within a very short time, I had become a phony expert on the subject. Before I began reading, I didn't know a Ouija board from a game of Scrabble.

All the while John was talking about the problems of researching the paranormal, my own thoughts kept fading in and out. Several times, I caught myself nodding in agreement over the wrong thing. I had a hard time concentrating on our discussion. For the first time since we'd been together our conversation seemed strangely forced. It was as if neither one of us was saying what we were really thinking. I had to keep reminding myself that these thoughts were probably just the product of my over-active imagination, but I still couldn't shake that self-conscious feeling. Even when John had asked me questions that were perfectly normal I had trouble responding. They were questions like: What did I do on my trip? Did I meet any interesting people?

Did I get along with the crew? I read something more into them. I felt as if he were trying to find out if I had met a guy. Maybe I was just projecting my own feelings of wanting to know what *he* did since our last meeting.

Thoughts kept running through my mind. Even if we were attracted to each other, it would never go anywhere. There was just too much time and space separating us. We didn't speak the same language, except when discussing the ghost. He was a writer. The only thing I ever wrote were college term papers, which were about as inspiring as airsick bags. John was a constant worrier, a hypochondriac, and often seemed to be insecure. At the same time he was overconfident and persistent, with a journalistic directness that sometimes chafed. But in spite of his flaws, he was the most irritatingly attractive character I'd ever known.

I didn't know what Arthur Ford's former house was going to look like. When we pulled up the driveway, it failed to meet my expectations. I was looking forward to a house more or less styled after the *Addams Family*, maybe with a moat or postern gate. I wasn't expecting a rather large, modern, rambling ranch-style structure.

Susan Graham, Patricia's mother, greeted us at the door. John declined an invitation to come in. It was late. He wanted to get back to the Marriott and get a good night's rest.

Once inside, Susan was cordial. She understood my doubts and hesitations and tried to make me feel comfortable. There was no one else there. She explained that the rest of the class would arrive the next day.

Before she showed me to my room, we spent

about twenty minutes chatting. I learned that she had been a close friend of Arthur Ford. After he died, he had left the house to her. Since that time, Patricia and Bud had been holding their weekend retreats here. I could see why. It was a good-sized home, with four bedrooms and three bathrooms, a spacious living room, and a complete library. There was no moat outside, but a large oblong swimming pool.

Even though it was late, I had a hard time falling asleep. I kept wondering what would happen over the next three days. John had told me at dinner that when he talked to Patricia, she told him that the course could lead to three things: increased sensitivity and awareness; development of psychic ability; and even progress into actual mediumship.

Susan gave me some brochures, and before I went to sleep, I leafed through them. One of the booklets explained what they called "the new mediumship" and how it worked:

". . . a highly ethical person who causes himself to become a conscious, spiritual and psychic channel. One who can, without prior knowledge of the person's life, background or problems, pick up feeling through which information and impressions come from a higher source than himself. The medium conveys this information through the use of his spiritual development to bring to that person an awareness and understanding of his physical, emotional and spiritual needs and potential. This aids in solving problems, resolving conflicts, answering questions and determining aspirations."

I thought if by some quirk of nature I ever developed into a medium, that would certainly solve a problem. If there was this ghost, Don Repo, and he was really communicating with the pilots, then why couldn't he communicate with me? John might believe me if I could gather enough evidence. But that was all fantasy. Here I was about to take a course that, according to Patricia, could possibly make me become a channel. And here I was with one lousy psychic experience, jumping into a field I really knew nothing about. In fact, the whole premise of mediumship was that you believed in life after death. I didn't know what I believed in. How could I possibly become a channel for something I wasn't sure about?

In spite of my uneasiness, I continued to read. "The spiritual development of a medium is not necessarily embellished with any significant act of birth or heritage. It is something every person has the ability to develop, and to use to one degree or another. We are not mystics. Most have never been blessed with any great vision of past or future events."

I was glad that I had read on. That was something I could relate to. I was no mystic. I was wondering if the others in the class were going to be like me, a novice. Or maybe they would be the Geller or Chambers or Manning types? Well, even if they were, I might learn something. Just what, I wasn't exactly sure of.

I was used to being with various types of people. I could adjust to anything for just three days. I was also wondering what the food would be like. John had commented about that while driving me here. He said that it would probably be comparable to a Howard Johnson's: never bad, never good, always mediocre. I had once flown with a girl who told me about an "ashram" that she went to over a weekend.

I took it to be something like a cross between a Jesuit seminary and a house of correction. They served rice and variations thereon, for three solid days. The purpose of the ashram was to get in tune with yourself. They apparently chanted and meditated themselves to a quiet frenzy the whole time. When they weren't doing that, they had a choice of cleaning the commune or weeding the garden. I was grateful that Arthur's house looked spic and span.

As I continued to read, I came across one of Arthur Ford's thoughts on spiritualism: "I always resent it when people speak of Spiritualists in a sort of sneering and unpleasant manner. Every man in the world is a Spiritualist if he is not a materialist. It's a perfectly good philosophical term. I am a Spiritualist because I believe in the spirit. No matter what name you wear, whether you are a Methodist or a Catholic or a Buddhist, if you have any conception of God or spiritual quality that doesn't perish at death, you are in a true sense a Spiritualist. The alternative is to be a materialist and depend only on the things that you can see and hear and touch." Although I didn't believe in an anthropomorphic God, I have always felt that there was some sort of great creative force in the universe, that kept the whole thing nailed together. So in that case, I was a Spiritualist, and didn't even know it. At least, according to Arthur Ford.

The next morning I was the last to join the group at the breakfast table. From one quick glance, everybody looked pretty normal. There were no saffron robes or chanting. I took a seat between a rather large-framed man in his early forties and a young woman probably in her early twenties. The girl introduced herself as Marlene.* We began to talk.

She told me that she was a nurse and she thought this course might enhance her ability to help patients. Later, I learned that her husband was a doctor and he was also planning to go through the course. The man on my right was named Charles.* He was a Protestant minister. He felt that if he could get more insight, it could possibly aid him in his counseling. Directly across the table was a striking-looking woman, from a socially prominent family. Seated next to her was a grandfather-type man who said he was semi-retired and living in the Keys. At the opposite end of the table was a schoolteacher, and next to her a builder.

The schoolteacher's name was Nancy.* It was her second time through the course. She explained that she got so much out of it the first time, she just decided to repeat it. That sounded strange to me. I was thinking that maybe it didn't work the first time. I immediately took to Nancy. She was vivacious and perceptive and constantly cracking jokes. We all kept quizzing her on what would be happening over the next three days. She was purposely evasive. She told us to wait and see.

So, the group was a mixed bag. It was very hard to believe that these people were all interested in a course that would eventually lead to mediumship. It seemed such a radical measure. I was thinking that maybe they knew something I didn't.

I was glad that the cook wasn't a health nut. I hated seeds and wheat germ almost as much as John hated eggplant. We were served grapefruit, bacon and eggs. There was nothing spiritual about it. By the time we left the table, we were all pretty stuffed and well acquainted. I no longer had that feeling of being alone.

After breakfast, we drifted into the living room.

There were several large sofas and chairs scattered around. We could sit anywhere. From the looks of the group, we could have been preparing for a Tupperware Party.

Patricia was standing in the center of the room. She appeared confident, a marked contrast to the rest of us. After placing a set of large charts on an easel, she began with a brief orientation.

What I gathered from the introduction was that all of us had capacities that we didn't use. Capacities that went far beyond the normal senses and apply reservoirs of untapped energy to our daily lives.

This was an advanced class, Patricia explained, for those who had shown more than the usual sensitivity and demonstrated an ability to reach these levels of energy. She explained that most people didn't realize they were psychic. Some of us had more capacity than others, just as some were better artists or piano players. The job was to let ourselves open up and remove certain blocks, blocks that would keep us from going beyond the limits of our five senses.

The most sensitive of those who tapped into this pool of energy were natural mediums, who developed in spite of themselves. In a sense, everyone had a touch of this capacity in him: dreams that coincided with future events; information that came spontaneously from an unknown source; the ability to heal; even direct messages from those who had died. The course we were all being introduced to would put us on the track to help others and to help ourselves to a greater and more creative potential.

My experience at the séance had convinced me that there might be some truth to what Patricia was saying. Where had those specific names come from during the Miami séance, names that I had never heard before in my life? Could further development here actually help in finding out the how and why of these strange appearances of Don Repo? It all seemed ridiculous—and yet, I wondered. Could two pilots be that wrong?

Neither John nor I knew. But John's theory was to try everything to learn more about the whole field of parapsychology and mediumship. If there was *anything* to the Ghost of Flight 401, at least a clue might be found here.

Patricia went on to talk about "extended sense perception." She explained this as going one step beyond the normal senses, invading the higher consciousness so that you have access to past, present, and future information. The school was offering this method to those who had shown a marked degree of awareness and sensitivity. Somehow I didn't feel as if I deserved the rating. I couldn't justify how one experience would qualify me for this advanced course. Maybe I had been accepted because they knew I was researching.

Patricia went on to say that the purpose of the class was not really to bring people into the psychic area. The idea of the course was to teach a method of moving into your higher energy field, and reaching out to areas seldom used, so that sense perception was increased. This would enable us to have increased rapport with anyone we were dealing with.

Patricia explained that during the next three days, we would be put through a series of exercises. She said that this was a technique for breaking down the "blocks." During that time, both she and Bud would be closely monitoring our results. She reminded us that they were not judging us. They would be helping in areas where we appeared weak.

I was anxious to find out where in the world all this would lead. I thought back several months to the time John and I had gone out into the deepest part of the Everglades to visit the scene of the crash.

We did this for two reasons. The first was to study the site in order to report on it accurately. The other reason was to attempt an experiment involving "psychometry" that Patricia had suggested.

According to Patricia, it was possible for a trained psychic to hold an object and pick up on its vibrations. This, they said, was called "psychometry" or "object reading." From the vibrations of the object, mediums were supposed to be able to obtain information not otherwise known to them. The theory was that a single object could possibly tell a whole story.

John and I were after clues, clues that could possibly give us some direct evidential information regarding the crash or the reappearances of Don Repo. Neither of us really was convinced that all this would bring any results. We were just working on John's favorite theory: Try anything once. I think he pictured himself as sort of a Sherlock Holmes.

On this advice, John and I had hired an airboat to take us through the flat, junglelike river of grass to the scene of the crash. The airboat looked a little like a three-tier erector set. The driver, was actually doing us a favor. His normal job was in electronics, but his first love was frog hunting and the Everglades was a haven for them. The driver, obviously, wasn't used to escorting tourists through the dense jungle. The tourist boats move at about 15 miles an hour. This guy opened it up to around 50 miles an hour, nearly top speed.

Before we left, we had lunch in a small Indian restaurant on the Tamiami Trail, where we discussed what our objective was over a hamburger and coffee. The driver told us that he knew exactly where the debris of the L-1011 lay. He predicted that it would take us about thirty minutes to get there. He was right. Exactly half an hour after we launched the fourteen-foot-high hunk of metal into the dense swamp, we arrived at our destination.

John climbed down from the third-floor saddle-seat first. Then Glen leaped from the middle section where the controls were. Hesitantly, I stepped out into the muck from my perch on the ground floor.

It was worse than eerie and depressing. Strewn as far as our eyes could see were remnants of that tragic night. Sprouting out from beneath the muddy water were torn pieces of the wrecked fuselage. The odor of jet fuel still permeated the air. The area smelled like an airport. John pulled part of an arm-rest section from a passenger's seat out of the muck. It was festooned with slime and sawgrass. It read: *Push for comfort, music, lights.* From just beneath the water I fished out an empty plastic credit-card holder, probably from someone's wallet.

Much of the aircraft was still submerged. Little things were sprinkled around: the leather magazine covers, plastic glasses with the airline logo, parts of the galley. These were the kinds of things I handled every day. The feeling of the tragedy was overwhelming.

I thought back three years to the night of the crash. I tried to imagine what it must have been like for the passengers and stewardesses who were clumping around in the blackness, searching for survivors. I thought about the brave stewardess who tried to keep up the morale until help arrived. She did it with Christmas carols. I thought about how I might have reacted in a similar crisis. I wasn't sure. I thought about the families and friends of those on board, waiting helplessly for news of their safety. But mostly I thought about that arm rest with those words written on it: *Push for comfort, music, lights.* That arm rest summed up the whole guts of the story—the fragility of life.

John and I carefully put twelve objects into separate heavy brown envelopes. As a control, John put a small part from a boat into an envelope. Later, John delivered the envelopes to Patricia. She then handed them over to a group of students.

The students sat in a circle, each clutching a brown bag. Their eyes were closed. They looked almost like they were about to fall asleep. After about ten minutes Patricia instructed them to write down the information they had received. One result was incredible:

AN AIRPLANE THAT LANDS IN WATER.
A MISSING PERSON
FEEL AS IF I AM CLOSE TO THE AIRPORT, CLOSE TO
A CANAL
I SEE LIGHTS, LIKE THOSE OF AN AIRPORT, THEN I
DON'T SEE THEM ANYMORE
FEEL A PAIN IN THE FOREHEAD AND EYES
THERE IS A VERY RESTLESS SPIRIT AT THE CRASH
SITE AND WILL NOT REST UNTIL HIS MOTHER
KNOWS ABOUT SPIRITUAL THINGS. SHE TOLD
HIM BUT HE DIDN'T BELIEVE HER. NOW HE DOES.
I SEE LIGHT AS IF I AM NEAR AN AIRPORT, THEN I
DON'T SEE THEM.

I FEEL A PAIN IN THE FACE, A SICK FEELING
TWO PLANES AT NIGHT, ONE FOLLOWING
ANOTHER
MALE VOICE SAYING MY MOTHER TOLD ME
ABOUT THIS BUT I DIDN'T BELIEVE HER. SHE
MUST STOP WORKING SO HARD AND SHE MUST
STOP WORRYING SO MUCH
I HAVE SEEN THE LIGHT . . . NOW I BELIEVE.
SOMEBODY MUST TELL HER
PLEASE TELL HER NOT TO CRY. I BELIEVE.

In spite of this and several other rather remarkable "object readings," John was still not satisfied. He wanted more direct evidential information. In fact, that is how the Miami séance had finally came about. Patricia had invited us to sit in on that first séance in an attempt to get more specific information.

Now, as I thought back, I wondered if going out to the crash site had anything to do with my receiving those names. Could I have touched anything connected with them?

I would never know the answers to that. But what I would discover would go beyond the "object readings," the first Miami séance, and beyond the four walls of the classroom to which I was now confined.

CHAPTER VII

THE CLASSROOM WAS actually becoming less confining. We were about to learn how to stretch mental muscles we had never used before. Patricia told us the perceptions of each person would be stretched and extended through a form of meditation. Each of us would be taken into our highest possible consciousness. There, it was hoped, we would experience the energies of that consciousness, so that the flow of information could easily come through to help in everyday life.

I thought I could really use something like that in my job. Many times I would encounter passengers who were extremely difficult to deal with. The Northwest manual covered everything from beverage usage forms to landing announcements in Cantonese, Japanese, and Korean. That's the one beauty in having the operations manual to abide by. The instructions were so explicit that you never needed to worry about unusual situations. Except, the manual was woefully skimpy when it came to cabin attendants reaching into their higher consciousness in order to deal with unhappy passengers.

Ours just said something about us being expected to be diplomatic and tactful with all passengers. It went on to say that when unusual or difficult situations arose, the senior attendant should make every possible effort to solve the problem. And all cabin attendants should receive passenger complaints graciously.

That was the trouble with airlines. The person who perpetrated that manual didn't have to deal with people in lump lots. He had no idea what it was like to serve hundreds of meals and pour endless amounts of Coke and dispose of scores of barf bags, all in a day's work. He didn't know what it was like for a passenger to hand you a twenty-dollar bill for a dollar-fifty drink. He didn't know what it was like to want to Karate-chop an innocent old lady, just because she wanted to know if she'd make her connection to Butte, Montana, before we'd left the ground in Anchorage. Then I thought to myself, if all I got out of these three days is the ability to "tune in" to what Patricia called the "flow" and maintain a positive attitude, I would be happy. I suddenly felt selfish—I was supposed to be taking the course for impersonal reasons. I was there for research.

Patricia handed the rest of the session over to Bud. He began to explain more about the course. He said that most people who take this advanced course already believe that there is something out there. Most don't know what, but they want to learn how to see more than just what they are seeing with their physical eyes. Sort of like opening up your psychic vision. "For example," he said, "if you just had a belief system that limited you to being born, going to school, getting married, and dying, that would be pretty depressing. We're going to try here to help you to unfold your higher consciousness and see who you really are." He went on to say that everybody is spiritual and everybody has some vision. He repeated what Patricia had said about breaking down these blocks that we have built up. It is getting to that essence, the soul or the spirit, or whatever you want to call it. It is all the same thing.

I was relieved that they weren't going to get off on a religious kick. If anything, the course was more or less based on the Eastern philosophy of the "Oneness."

Although he went on to say that everybody there had the potential of becoming a medium, this did not mean that on Sunday we would all be turned loose to go and hang a plaque on a door: *Readings Here.* The majority of people who went through this course never gave readings. The school's purpose was to help us achieve our highest potential, whatever that may be. And that could mean counseling, or coping in our jobs, or even using this flow of information to contact the "other side." He reminded us that we would be the judge of how we wanted to use it.

Bud stressed that they were in no way working against religion. He said most religions were based on the premise that we survived death. That is where a lot of people have trouble with the organized religions they can't accept on faith alone. All mediumship did was to provide living evidence of the foundation that most religion rested on. Mediums, he said, were merely putting religion to the ultimate test.

But, he said, for those of us who chose not to believe in life after death, fine. There were no ground rules here, except to follow along with the exercises and try not to block whatever you feel. In other words, for the next three days we were to just try to express our feelings without using our intellect. I was beginning to wonder where John was. It was nearly eleven o'clock. I was sure he was expecting to find me in the middle of a bunch of zombies, wearing a turban, and playing poker with a deck of Tarot cards.

Immediately following the orientation, Patricia began handing out small green cards. They weren't Tarot cards. I was glad to see. Bud explained that we were about to have our first exercise. He told us to write down on the green card what we thought was going to happen to us when we died. My first impulse was to jot down something philosophical and flowery, just so I would appear "deep." But I resisted the temptation. I wrote:

"Lately, I've given much thought to this question. However, I have never been able to come up with an answer that would even in the slightest way satisfy me. I hope after these three days to gain some sort of insight into a spiritual life, if there really is such a thing."

After several minutes the cards were collected. I felt as if I were back in school.

John arrived just before lunch. He had been tied up at the University of Miami, where he was completing his oceanography research. When John walked into the room, I could tell by his expression that he wasn't expecting such a straight-looking group. I told him that I had been taking copious notes and began to fill him in a little on the morning session. Then he took a seat on the sidelines, and tried to fade into the woodwork.

After the green cards, we did what Patricia called "tuning in." We all sat around a large circle. We were instructed to look into the eyes of the person next to us and to tell him what we saw. Patricia said that this was the beginning of breaking down the blocks. It was a technique to get into harmony with the higher realms. Bud told us to imagine ourselves as human television sets. In the physical realm, our bodies were able to pick up certain frequencies, but through this exercise, we would learn to increase our capacity for greater reception in the higher realm. We were merely "tuning in" to a different rate of vibration.

I felt very queasy with this exercise. It reminded me of a "rap-and-touch" session technique that was popular in California. When it was my turn to look into my partner's eyes, I began to become inarticulate, self-conscious, and embarrassed. I felt as if I were invading private areas. I knew the reason behind the exercise but I still felt inhibited.

I mentioned how I felt about that exercise. Patricia reassured me that it was a natural reaction and by the end of the first day I would feel more at ease. Bud explained that all of the methods they used were to aid us in breaking through the physical barriers. We could then reach a level that didn't deal with the physical feelings such as embarrassment and self-consciousness.

I glanced over to where John was sitting. He was squinting quizzically. I could tell he was taking in every word. In fact, I had asked Bud and Patricia about that exercise mainly for John's benefit. I wanted him to know that I hadn't had a mystical experience yet, not by any means.

Patricia began to explain with a series of charts how we would eventually reach this high level. She said it was a four-step process, beginning with level one.

Level one was the physical vibration. She pointed to the flip chart on the easel. It was an illustration of a man who lived and operated on this lower plane. This man was only aware of his surroundings, his opinions, his views. He was totally self-centered.

She then flipped the chart to the second level. It was the same illustration, except that this time he was captioned as being one step above the physical. This person was sensitive to his surroundings plus those of other people, but he was not yet aware of the psychic world. Creativity, perception, and sensitivity were housed in this level. This person would look at you and make a character evaluation by the lines in your face or the clothes on your back. He would have the potential of being a good counselor or schoolteacher.

The third level showed the same man, but this time he was focused on the psychic and spirit world which, Patricia explained, are one and the same. They came from the same vibration, which was one step away from the physical (or level two). This level is often called the astral plane. You could believe in the psychic world, but not believe in life after death. In this psychic world, you could read past, present and future events. It was where the often-reported manifestations came from. When we died, we were purported to go to the astral world. This world was supposed to be everything that was related to the physical. I guessed this would be the area that Don Repo would come from, if there were any truth to the story. Still, this level stuff all sounded so pat. It reminded me of the Heaven, Hell, and Purgatory scene I left back in Catholic school.

The charts may have been ethereal, but my appetite was not. It was nearly one o'clock and my physical body couldn't transcend its earthly cravings. I was starved. After about fifteen minutes of questions and answers on levels one through three, it was finally time to eat. After lunch, Patricia would discuss the final level, level four.

John joined us for lunch. It was impossible for us to talk alone. I didn't want those in the group to feel as if they were being observed under a microscope. They weren't. John was merely auditing the course to observe how I would develop psychically. We were served a variety of sandwiches, with all the trimmings of cole slaw, potato salad, and cottage cheese. There were no cocktails before or during lunch. It didn't go unnoticed. John leaned over and quietly muttered, "The liquor flows like glue around here." He enjoyed his before-lunch cocktail almost as much as his after-dinner cigarette.

Even though the morning session made us all pretty uneasy, the feeling wore off during lunch. We had a common bond—we all felt inadequate. That is, everybody except Nancy. Nancy kept telling us that the course got better. But when we asked her when and how, she'd just repeat, "Wait and see." Then she would go on about something completely unrelated to the psychic. Finally, halfway through lunch, I said, "Nancy, seriously, what is it like to give a psychic reading to somebody? Does the information really flow through, as Patricia said?" Suddenly, a totally sober expression came over her. I thought to myself: *For once, I'm going to get a straight answer.* She began:

"I recently had an elderly gentleman golfer come for a reading. He asked me if I could contact his best friend, Harry, who had recently passed over. He wanted me to ask Harry if they have golf courses on the other side."

At that point Nancy stopped and looked at each one of us for our reaction. There was dead silence.

She went on, "I told the man that I felt as if I had made contact with Harry and the news came in two parts. The man nodded and asked me to give him the good news first."

Nancy stopped again. She seemed to enjoy keeping us in suspense as long as possible.

"Come on, Nancy. On with it," I said.

She continued, "I told the man that his friend, Harry, said that the golf courses are better than anything he has ever seen on earth. They made Boca Raton's course look like a city dump. Then I said to the man, 'Are you ready for the bad news?' He was hesitant, but nodded."

Nancy stopped the story for the third time to make sure she had our undivided attention. She did.

She continued, "The bad news is that you'll be teeing off next Sunday at 9:30." And on that note, she cracked up. Nancy was delightfully hopeless.

In spite of her sense of humor, Nancy later revealed that she was very serious about the whole field, but she didn't want to jump ahead of Patricia and Bud. She said something about not having words adequate enough to express the total experience. She went on to say that the mediumship course was not one that lent itself easily to a conventional description. Besides, she said, each person experiences something entirely different. She didn't want to influence us with her own experience. In spite of her rational explanation, I still wondered why she was holding back the esoteric knowledge.

Nancy's golf story was, of course, a joke. But

later I learned of two remarkable stories having to do with life after death. The accounts were especially interesting because they were both direct personal experiences of medical scientists.

Dr. Elisabeth Kübler-Ross, the noted neuropsychiatrist, had spent twenty-five years of her practice studying dying patients. According to a story published in *Newsweek* and several newspapers, several years after she had decided to drop that sort of study, a woman entered her office. Dr. Kübler-Ross immediately recognized the woman as a patient who had died six months earlier. The woman sat down across from Dr. Kübler-Ross's desk and told her that she was disappointed in the doctor's decision to give up studying dying patients.

Dr. Kübler-Ross's thoughts flashed back to all the times she had counseled patients who had reported seeing such apparitions. She conducted a quick reality test, asking the woman to write down her name and address. The patient did so, and then walked right out the door.

Startled, Dr. Kübler-Ross verified the slip of paper against other documents signed by the former patient. The signatures were identical. Elisabeth Kübler-Ross is now, incidentally, lecturing all over the world on her convictions of the reality of life after death. If I had known about Dr. Kübler-Ross's studies before this course, I probably would have been more open to what Patricia was talking about. It was just so hard to conceive of an actual life in another dimension—if for no other reason than it would probably be too crowded up there.

John had briefly mentioned a theory of H. H. Price, Professor of Logic at Oxford, that partially answered this question. Price's theory was that it is possible we live after death in an image world, much as we do in dreams. The scenery here, just as in dreams, could shift faster than the speed of light and wouldn't require any *real* real estate, as John put it. Therefore, there wouldn't need to be any "crowding." We could, under this idea at least, create our space—and it could be unlimited.

I asked John if he believed Price's theory. He told me, "It's the first rational explanation I've run across that makes it even possible to imagine how we could have a geography that didn't take up any space. Dreams are real until we wake up and find that they're not." This was interesting food for thought, but I would have to give this a lot more study.

I was also to discover that another psychiatrist had a paranormal experience. In fact, Dr. George Ritchie's own account of life after death had inspired Dr. Raymond A. Moody to write his bestseller, *Life-After-Life*. Dr. Moody even dedicated the book to him.

In 1943, when Dr. Ritchie was in the service, he was selected to go to the University of Virginia Medical School. He said that at that time in his life, he felt as if he had the world by the tail. By the time he reached the age of twenty-five, he was sure he would have a home on the beach and a Cadillac in his garage. However, five days before he was to enter medical school, he landed in the hospital with an upper respiratory infection. By 3 A.M., he felt terrible. He asked the ward boy what his temperature was and discovered that it was 106°.

The ward boy ran for the doctor. A chest X-ray was immediately ordered for Ritchie.

Ritchie said that the last thing he could remember was the X-ray. Later, he found out that he had been pronounced dead. There was no pulse, no blood pressure. He had "died" from double lobar pneumonia. The ward boy was ordered to prepare him for the morgue. Ten minutes after he had been declared dead, another doctor came in and confirmed it. Somehow the ward boy insisted that they try giving him a shot of adrenalin. This was considered highly dangerous because it could create a living vegetable. But the heart started almost immediately.

Recalling his terrifying experience, Ritchie told later what happened during the time he "died."

"I sat up on the side of my bed, upset that I would miss my train back to Richmond. What I wasn't prepared for was looking back and seeing myself lying there. I felt myself rise from the foot of the bed and walk across the corridor. I saw a ward boy rolling a stretcher down it and I walked right through the stretcher and out the hospital door. I seemed to travel at the speed of sound. I was determined to get to Richmond. I found myself lying on the street next to an illuminated cafe. Soldiers passed me. I tried to speak but they walked right through me.

He went on to report that he had left his body back on the bed. Suddenly, he realized that if a ward boy or the man on the street hadn't seen him and passed right through him, something was wrong. He simply had to go back and pick up his body. But he couldn't remember what room he was in and the hospital had over three thousand beds.

Dr. Ritchie continues his description:

It was a real physical identity crisis. After what seemed like hours, I found my body. But the sheet was pulled up over my head. I could tell because my hand was sticking out and my fraternity ring with a chipped stone was still on my hand. I noticed that my hand was very blue. I was horrified. I then sat on the bed and tried to pull the sheet off my body. But I failed.

The situation hit Dr. Ritchie like a ton of bricks. He knew that it must be death. He felt cheated and sorry for himself. Then he looked up and noticed a small 15-watt bulb in the room. He wanted to get out of there.

"I hated sitting beside my dead body," his report goes on. "Then suddenly the little light increased in brightness—as brilliant as a welder's torch.

"Just then three things happened simultaneously," he continues. "A 'form' stepped out of the light. The form said to me through telepathy: You are in the presence of the Son of God. Then the walls of the room disappeared. I saw my whole life flash before me. All the minute details."

Ritchie said that his religious training had taught him that you either go to Heaven or Hell. But, he said, this wasn't the truth. The form he saw before him was not like the Bible-school Jesus. It was the most powerful figure imaginable. He had never been in the presence of someone who radiated such total love.

Ritchie was then led to a large city by this powerful being. He saw through spiritual eyes. He was led to what looked like a red-light district. Men were sitting at bars, but he said he could see low spirit forms trying to steal their drinks. Their hands, however, would go right through the glasses. Some spirits were waiting for men to pass out, so that they could get inside their bodies.

Ritchie was given no instructions. He was just told to observe and to make his own conclusions. He then moved into a higher realm, where there was beautiful music. This realm set aside all prejudices, racial and religious. He saw huge libraries that housed all the holy books of the universe.

Finally, the figure that Ritchie described as Christ opened up still another realm. Here there were many beings but they were in the likeness of Christ himself.

The next thing he remembered was that he woke up in the hospital back in his own body. Ritchie says that this experience was so powerful to him that he has finally made the decision to give up his practice to convince people of the reality of life after death.

These two accounts were impressive in themselves. But I found them doubly intriguing because I could clearly see the similarities between the Kübler-Ross, the Ritchie case, and the Repo reports.

For instance, the patient who had manifested in Dr. Kübler-Ross's office was intent on telling the doctor that the deathbed study was important. The patient urged her not to give it up. This reported appearance was closely related to one of Don Repo's alleged manifestations. Repo was said to have warned correctly about a fire in No. 3 engine in a plane over Mexico City. He had apparently appeared as a full-bodied apparition in front of a stewardess and second officer. The lady patient had appeared as a full-bodied apparition in front of her doctor. Both of these apparitions had used direct audio contact.

The Ritchie and Repo cases also had their similarities. Both involved crisis situations. Ritchie had "died" suddenly without time to prepare for his death, just as Repo had died. Ritchie had indicated that his experience showed him that many of those who had died seemed to want to return to their former lives. Then, if what crew members had reported were true, Don Repo would fall into the sort of thing Ritchie had encountered. Would it be possible that Repo was unable to accept that he was dead? Did he love the L-1011 so much that he couldn't let go? If so, would this also agree with Manning's and the Chamberses' theory on "soul rescue"? They said they had been helping Repo to realize that he was no longer a physical being and were guiding him on to his further development. We would learn the answers to those questions in the months that followed.

The highlight of the three-day course was reaching the fourth level, the level Patricia and Bud called our "Spiritual Society." Nancy was right in not telling us about her experience. It was difficult to verbalize.

The best way to describe the Spiritual Society is to compare it to a time in your life when you felt inspired or guided, or felt keenly in tune with the universe, at one with it. There are times, rare as they are, when a person can feel for a moment that he knew everything, when he might write a beautiful poem, or plant a fantastic garden, or work out the perfect solution to a problem.

In a sense, everybody is creative and has had moments like that. The theory is that in your Spiritual Society were distinct personalities who had progressed from the third level, the astral or psychic level, to become spiritual teachers. They were available to those who recognized them for protection, creative inspiration and spiritual insight, direction, and guidance. They had, if the theory were true, come up from the astral level—the level we are purported to go to when we die.

We each have our own Spiritual Society which acts as guide. The difference between meditation and reaching your Spiritual Society is that in meditation you attempt to reach a state of calm or better insight. But in going to your Spiritual Society, you're saying: "Use me as a channel."

You try to release yourself completely. For instance, when you give psychic readings, you're asking your Spiritual Society to filter through you information that will benefit the person you're trying to help. Your Spiritual Society will be the judge of what type of information is needed and how the person you hope to aid can best achieve his full potential. The important thing for the medium to keep in mind is that you must trust this information. That takes faith.

All this sounded very exalted when I learned it, and in fact, it was. It was also very hard to absorb and understand. Were there really distinct personalities on a plane beyond us, who were willing to help if we could get through to them? Had they really worked their way up from the astral level, where they had gone when they died? If that were the case, was this the spiritual progress and development that the Chamberses and Manning had talked about when they encouraged Don Repo to become less earthbound? Were these individuals, if they were individuals, one more step on the way to God?

And just who were they, anyway? I was a little wary of things like tin gods, sitting on top of Mount Olympus. Could these gods trickle down to ordinary mortals who had just died, on the lower astral level, so that a channel could be opened up for communication with them, through a still-living medium? How could actual facts come through, facts that could be verified? It all left me a little dizzy. But as I was to learn later, it actually worked.

On the third day Patricia or Bud took each one of us separately to this higher level of consciousness. There was really nothing spooky about it. Patricia took me into a quiet part of the house and instructed me to relax, void my mind of all thoughts, and take a few deep breaths, inhaling peaceful energy and exhaling calm. Then she said to breathe very naturally and feel myself lifting, just as if I were on a cloud, feeling lighter and lighter.

This procedure must have lasted for about fifteen minutes. All the while, Patricia was saying that she was using her energies to help me reach this elusive fourth level. It was actually a deep form of meditation, which could also be considered a form of hypnosis.

Patricia told me that it would be in this state of consciousness that I would become attuned to and acquainted with other forces we don't normally see. She explained that the forces are around all of us all the time, but few of us realize it. She said she was sort of introducing me to this Spiritual Society. The meditation lasted roughly an hour. Immediately following it, I was instructed to go into my bedroom and write down as clearly and as accurately as possible what I had experienced. I wrote:

> I never really believed that I could ever achieve a feeling that the Buddhists speak of as nirvana, a mental state of perfect peace and harmony. But, I did. I seemed to lose all my earthly desires and passions. I have always felt as if I were too much emerged in my own physical reality—my own ego—to experience anything mystical. It was as if I had climbed out of my body and blended with everything around me. I lost my individual awareness but gained something much greater. I suddenly became aware of a force that was so powerful it transcended all words in *Webster's Unabridged*. I felt as if I were being encompassed by thousands of white lights. But at the same time, brilliant colors were swirling everywhere. Then, there was some sort of entities. Maybe they were spirits, encasing me with love and protection. I felt totally at home. I didn't want to leave. I knew that I had to. But, I also left knowing that I could return to my Spiritual Society for insight, guidance, and truth. I just knew that all this was right—this is where the "flow" came from.

After I finished pouring out my thoughts onto the large yellow card, I went to look for John. I found him sitting alone in the library with a book propped up on his lap. He was sound asleep. That is, until I gently but firmly shook his arm. He slowly opened his eyes. Then for a few seconds he just sat there staring up at me. Finally, he said, "Well, you *look* the same. What happened in your psychic bath?"

I handed him the yellow card to read. He read both sides rather quickly. Then he looked up at me, as if he were studying me for signs of brain damage. I didn't respond. He began to re-read, this time more slowly. Then he looked at me for a second time, but his expression was different. It was more of an impressed type of look.

"You really write that?" he asked.

"No," I said. "I hired a ghost writer."

"I didn't mean it that way," he said. "I meant that it just doesn't sound like any of your letters. It's so serious."

"That's because I was serious. Dead serious."

He nodded in half-agreement. "Did all that stuff really happen to you? The colors and spirits and all?" he asked.

"If it didn't really happen, I wouldn't have said that it did."

"I suppose, then, that you really had quite an experience," he said.

I couldn't believe that I was hearing correctly. That didn't sound like a Fuller comment. He seemed pliable, less contentious. There was a long pause, then he added, "Who do you suppose put the LSD in the dessert?"

"Very amusing," I said. I took the card from his lap, plopped down on the floor, and read it. "Okay," I said. "I must admit that it isn't in my usual style. Sorta soupy, huh?"

"No," John replied, "it's really touching." He looked as if he were deep in thought, before muttering, "Maybe, a little soupy."

John still didn't quite share my enthusiasm. I

really couldn't blame him. But I had to get my point across. "Well, John G. Fuller, there are a lotta things in life that are soupy. Just because something is soupy, that doesn't mean that it's not true."

"Well, it must be nice if you can have an experience like that," he said.

"You could, too. If you'd ever relax that journalistic bit."

— "I've got to remain objective. I'd lose my credibility." Then he reluctantly added, "If I have any credibility left after this ghost hunt."

"You could be a closet psychic. I would never tell anybody," I said.

"I could never be any kind of psychic," he said.

"You're thinking negative."

"Negative or not—what happens after this beautiful psychedelic trip of yours?" he asked.

"We go back over the charts, then we do some practice readings with the group. All of this is supposed to prepare us for the grand finale."

"I'm afraid to ask," he said. "What's the grand finale?"

"You don't have to ask," I said. "I'm about to tell you. Remember when Nancy kept avoiding telling us about what was to come?"

"Yeah," he said. "I thought it was because she was always telling funny stories."

"Wrong," I said. "If she had told us that on the last day we had to give psychic readings to five outsiders, we would have all split."

"Want to run that by me once again?" John said.

"Give psychic readings to five people."

"How do you feel about that?" he asked.

"I'm a little bit nervous but I'm going to try to not think about it until the time comes. You know, it may sound weird but I have a funny feeling that I'll be able to do it."

"I hope you're right," he said. "I also hope that this whole mediumship thing doesn't go to your head."

"What do you mean by that?" I said. "You're the one who thought it was a good idea to come here."

"I know," he said. "I just don't want you to change, to get all serious and heavy."

"You mean like take a trip to India? Contemplate Truth with a guru on a mountaintop? That kind of change?" I asked.

"Possibly." I felt as if he wanted to add something, but he didn't.

"John, I've got an idea."

"What's that?"

"We could both take a trip to India. Then we could get a Hertz Rent-a-Guru and meditate on the mountaintop together."

"It wouldn't work," he said.

"Why wouldn't it?"

"The Hertz Rent-a-Guru would fall in love with you and I would be left stranded without a researcher."

"You're assuming that it'll be a male guru," I said. "What if we got a female guru and the reverse happened? I would then be the one who was stranded."

"That would never happen," he said.

"Why not?"

"Because I'm too old for a guru."

"You're assuming that all gurus are young," I said.

"They have to be," he said. "If the wind and rice

doesn't get to them by the time they're twenty-eight, the mountain-climbing will."

"Well, even if you're right, gurus don't care about age. They have transcended all those ridiculous age hang-ups."

I could hear Patricia calling me from the living room. It was time to review the charts. Our guru game had come to an end, at least temporarily.

CHAPTER VIII

I WAS MORE than a little nervous the next day. The idea of facing five total strangers was almost frightening. I didn't quite know how I was going to attempt to bring to them an awareness of their needs and their potential. Was I *obligated* to do something like this? What if I tried and failed? And yet, that deeply moving experience I had had the day before gave me completely unwarranted confidence. The only other reassuring fact was that we all felt the same way: scared to death. We were assigned to different rooms. As the volunteer subjects came in, they were divided up among the students.

The first volunteer who was sent to me was a young man in his twenties. I, of course, had never met him and knew nothing about him. He came into the room and sat down opposite me. I asked him to relax, even though I was tense myself. I thought back to what Patricia told us earlier that morning: "You will be able to receive this information due to your spiritual development—you must trust your impressions and forget your conscious mind."

I held the young man's hand, as we had been instructed in class, "tuning in" to his vibrations. I thought back to that first day, when I had felt very embarrassed by the rap-and-touch-type session. I no longer felt that way. As I took his hand, I voided my mind and concentrated on reaching the fourth level, where that newly found Spiritual Society was supposed to reside. I was praying they—whoever "they" were—wouldn't let me down.

I altered my state of consciousness as we had been taught. I closed my eyes. I regulated my breathing. With every breath, I concentrated on lifting myself higher and higher. I silently asked that I be used as a conscious channel for information that would help this man.

All this took about three minutes. Then, suddenly, I began to get impressions. It was almost as if I were in a daydream. Clear images unrolled on my mental screen. My first thought-impression was of a large boat going under a drawbridge. I told him that I felt as if that boat meant something to him. He looked at me and slowly nodded yes.

In the beginning of the session, I had asked him to hold back any questions or information that could give me a conscious lead. This was important.

I recalled what we had read in our study sheet: "Unlike the psychiatrist, the medium does not want you to tell him your problems. The nature of mediumship is such that the problems usually become apparent without your ever mentioning them.

"Any questions by the visitor should be reserved until the end of the reading. Instruct the visitor not to block the contact between you and him by holding any questions in his mind. Many times they will be answered without his ever having to ask."

"If, during the reading, information being channeled through the medium does or does not have any meaning, ask the visitor to simply answer 'yes' or 'no.' If he is not sure, ask him to say 'I don't know.' Ask him to please not elaborate on the subject, as this may tend to change its significance."

I felt a strange impulse to tell the man that the boat was holding him back from pursuing his other talent as an artist. But I didn't. At first, I avoided telling him this. I didn't want to be responsible in any way for altering his life-style. I was wary of giving the wrong advice. I also felt as if I might be all wet. This could all be in my imagination.

But I continued to receive colorful images. In my mind's eye I say an easel with colors splashed all over it. I interpreted all this as his ability to draw. The feeling about his talent became so strong that I no longer held back. Rather than asking him if he had any talent, I trusted my strong feelings. I told him. Again he nodded. My conscious thoughts kept peeking through. Even though he was agreeing, I wanted to know exactly how close I was. Maybe he was agreeing, I thought, because he didn't want to hurt my feelings.

Without warning, I received two names. They were Douglas and David. I knew they weren't coming from my conscious mind. Maybe they were coming from this Spiritual Society? But I still had no idea how my Spiritual Society knew specific names like Douglas and David.

Receiving those names reminded me of that first séance when I had got those names of Flight 401 passengers. I felt that these names would mean something to my visitor. There was no other rational explanation. I asked him if Douglas and David meant anything to him. This time he didn't nod. His eyes filled up with tears. After a few seconds, he softly whispered yes. I had that same lightheaded feeling that I had that day at the library,

Elizabeth Fuller

when John and I read the passenger lists. Again, I
felt as if I were in a dream. Nothing seemed real. I
continued the reading. I told the young man that I
felt as if Douglas had died. Then a quick stream of
messages came to me. I can't explain how. I didn't
hear them. I didn't see them. They were not coming
from any of my five senses. I gave the messages in
the order that I received them. I just *knew* they were
right:

"Douglas wants you to know that he is happy
because you're going to marry his sister," I found
myself saying. "He is adamant about wanting his
sister and mother to know that he is not really dead.
He is alive, but in another realm. He said something
about David being with him. His last message is that
you should tell his mother about this visit. She
would understand. Tell her to stop crying over the
figurines. She must not ruin her life by mourning.
There is too much good she can do on earth."

As quickly and clearly as the flow came, that's
how fast it ended. The man still had tears in his eyes.

I couldn't possibly justify to myself how this
stream of words poured out of me. I knew the theory
behind meeting my Spiritual Society, but a practical
application of this seemed ludicrous. I was beginning to think that this "trip" was all in my imagination, especially after John's reaction. I was starting
to question if I really did experience what I wrote on
that yellow card. I could just have been reacting to a
situation. I knew that I was *supposed* to have an
incredible experience, so possibly, I could have con-
jured all this up unconsciously. It could have been
like a hypnotic suggestion.

Here, though, was a moment of truth. These were
facts, detailed facts. There were only three alterna-

tives: either I gave my visitor correct information, I had the most fantastic imagination, or I had flipped out. John, I'm sure, would go for No. 3.

When the visitor began to confirm these strange messages, I was stunned. He told me that Douglas was his best friend. He went on to say that they had both worked as crew on a charter boat together. Then two years earlier, Douglas was killed in a car crash on his way home from work. About a year later, my visitor had become engaged to Douglas's sister. The sister was just one year younger than Douglas. They were extremely close. The sister never really got over the sudden death of her brother. In fact, the visitor told me that the reason he was here was because his fiancée urged him to come. It was a long shot that possibly something concerning her brother might just come through. He told me that this information would be a great comfort to Douglas's family. I was more surprised than he was to discover that this information was true. I was pleased not for egoistic reasons, but because I felt as if I were able to do something to alleviate this family's grief.

David, he continued, was a mutual friend who was killed in the Vietnam War. They all went to the same high school. As far as the art work went, sketching was a hobby Douglas and he had both shared.

"In fact," he said, "we planned one day on taking art lessons. Douglas had always kidded me about doing portraits, instead of working on the boat. He'd thought I was really good at drawing people." I missed on one thing I had said: he did not understand the figurine part of the message. But so much had been accurate that I was starting to believe in the reality of communication with the "other side."

I did four more readings in a similar manner. The content of the readings varied but the flow was consistent.

After each reading, the volunteer subject went into the library and evaluated the reading given him or her by answering questions rating the experience, "good, fair, poor," and so on. The purpose of the evaluation was to clinically test our capacities as channels.

We were told that we were required to do these readings to prove to ourselves that this "flow" really existed and that it was there for us to use. I'm sure that I would have never had the confidence to give a first reading unless required to. In fact, I probably would have chalked up those three days as just a pleasant experience—nothing more.

When I learned how I rated on the score sheets, I was startled. I was also surprised to discover that in all of my five readings, there was evidence of communication with the "other side."

I couldn't take any personal credit for the accuracy of my readings, of course. I was merely acting as a channel to give help and guidance to others. The "trip" the day before had been a beautiful experience, but the readings were the confirmation I needed. They confirmed to me that I really must have reached my Spiritual Society, regardless of how ridiculous that phrase sounded. Some of the information that came through in those five readings may have been trivial but the impact on me was profound.

The readings were over by noon of the last day. John and I took a walk around the block before the farewell lunch at the school.

"All right. Out with it. How did you do on this reading business?" he asked.

"You won't believe it," I said. "I mean you *really* won't believe it. You know that trip they put us through yesterday?"

"Yes. I know that trip. But I still don't understand it."

"The whole thing really works," I said. "The trip wasn't just in my imagination."

"Elizabeth, dear, you've got to be more specific."

"Well, that's what I'm about to tell you. During those five readings, I got real specifics. The kind you'll like. I got names, dates, places. They really came through."

"You keep saying how they 'come through,'" John said. "I just don't understand what that means."

"John, I don't *know.* All of a sudden I started getting all these names. I don't *know* how. I can't explain how. I just get them."

"This is always so vague," he said.

John was really starting to bug me. "Fuller, all I can tell you is that it's as if it's a gut reaction. It's not me talking. It's as if it's coming from somebody else. I just know 'they' are right."

"But can't you understand how hard it is for me to understand *this*?" he said.

"I suppose. But you're trying to ask me to explain something I don't even understand," I added. "Listen, I never even had a psychic experience before in my life. How do you think I feel?"

"You're wonderful, honest," he said. "But how do you know that you're not just kidding yourself?" he asked.

"Where would I get names and facts about people I hadn't known before?" I said. For the first time since I'd known John I realized that he was really kind of annoying. In one quick walk with him, I had forgotten everything I learned about being able to cope, being able to transcend my feelings of anger, hate. I wanted to let him have it.

"But doesn't it seem crazy that just because you take a short course in consciousness expansion you're able to do this?" he pressed.

"Yes, I have to admit it does sound crazy. It sounds crazier than crazy. But that's not the point. The point, for the hundredth time, is that I *did* it. Please, Fuller, try to accept that."

"Okay, at least you admit it sounds crazy," he said.

"I'll admit something else, too."

"What's that?" he asked.

"You're bugging me," I said.

"I'm sorry, Elizabeth." He put his arm around my shoulder and squeezed. "Go ahead. I'll be good."

"According to the Hayeses," I said, "we all showed psychic ability before the course. We were sort of like natural mediums, waiting to happen."

"Could anyone do anything like this?" John asked.

"I don't think so," I said. "You'd never let yourself go. You'd never believe it and you've got to believe it to do it."

"I'm not against believing it, but I mean . . ." His voice trailed off.

"Why would I make this up?" I said. "How do you explain how I got all that information in those readings?"

"That's what gets me," he said. "I don't know.

That's what I'm trying to find out." Then he added: "But how could anything like this work with investigating the Don Repo thing?"

"I would have never believed it possible before," I said, "but now I think it's worth a try. Why couldn't we try contacting Repo? Then we could maybe get some clues to if he really is appearing on the planes. And if Laura, Manning, and the Chamberses are really playing with a full deck."

"Well," John said. He wasn't very articulate at this point.

"I mean, I didn't believe them," I said. "I thought they were nuts. Now here I am, with the same sort of thing. And you're going to think I'm nuts too. I mean, you don't really even believe *me*." My fist was in a ready position. "I took this course, and now you think that I'm nuts."

"Hey, slow down," John said. "I don't think that you're nuts. But how is anybody going to . . . Let's assume for a minute that you think that you're in touch with some alleged message from Repo, right?"

"Right," I said

"Who's going to believe it? Even if you got something through?"

"Well, that's the problem," I said. "You're right about who's going to believe this. Really —who? Unless we could get specific information as I did in those five readings."

"What are the chances of that?" he asked. "I mean you happened to get something through on those tests, but—"

"First of all, I can't guarantee you anything. There are no guarantees. All I know is that trip seemed to open me up psychically."

"The whole thing is vague and unbelievable," he said.

"Vague or not, John, lay off, will you?"

"I'm sorry. I keep forgetting that you're touchy about this whole thing."

"I might as well try to use what I've learned, don't you think? Of course, I never came here believing that I'd ever walk through a wall, or anything. I was just coming here for...I don't know what I was coming here for."

"Well, I asked you to come here for one reason," he said. "I was hoping that you might learn something about the whole background. Because, obviously, this 401 story is tangled up with psychic phenomena. It's that simple."

"Well, where do we go from here?" I said. "Maybe try some experiments?"

"I'm not in a very experimental frame of mind," he said. "I'm starting to wish we hadn't gotten so deep into this."

"Look, John," I said. "I'm starting to think that this whole thing wasn't an accident. I mean like my meeting you on the flight to Edmonton."

"Take it easy," John said.

"No, I really am starting to think that. Because before I met you, I never had any psychic experiences."

"What's that got to do with it?" John asked.

"Maybe, just maybe," I said, "a force greater than the two of us arranged this whole meeting. Arranged for us to get together. Arranged for that first séance. Arranged for this course. Arranged for—"

"*Hold* on," John said. "I'm not going to let you

buy that. The most important thing in any kind of
story like this is not to let yourself go around the
bend."

"I haven't gone around the bend. Those readings
this morning proved it," I said.

"Okay, fine," he said. "I'm not against that. I'm
puzzled, but not against it. You don't understand.
How could anyone ever use material like this so
anybody will ever believe it? Even if something *did*
come through?"

"Are you willing to try something?" I asked.

"I've gone this far," he said. "What do you have
in mind?"

"Nancy suggested we try a Ouija board. She said
that it might be a good experiment in our situation.
You don't even have to be psychic to use it."

"Oh, come on," John said.

"You willing to buy one?" I asked.

"Knock it off," he said.

"I'm really serious," I said. He was walking faster
now, and I was getting out of breath. "Hey, Fuller,
do you want to slow those legs down a little?"

I was practically running to keep up with him,
before he slammed on the brakes. He changed the
subject from the Ouija board to how he jogged every
day when he was in Connecticut, and that if you're
going to walk, it's better to do it briskly, something
about the heart. Then he said something about vitamin B_6, and that nobody really knows what's good
for you. I didn't catch his point.

"Are you avoiding my question?" I asked.

"You mean about vitamin B_6 being any good for
you?"

"I don't care about vitamin B_6," I said. "I asked
you about buying a Ouija board."

"Well," he said. "I have to admit that I did see a Ouija board in action once. Up at a writers' colony that I went to in New Hampshire."

"So that's why you were avoiding my question," I said.

He ignored me. Then I added: "How's it supposed to work? I've never seen one."

"It's a board about the size of a desk blotter. It's got the full alphabet and numbers on it. There's a small indicator on three legs with a window in the center. When two people put their fingers lightly on that indicator, the thing moves," he said.

"Where does it move?" I asked.

"It moves to different letters on the alphabet. Sometimes," he added, "it even spells out words. Entire sentences."

"How can you be sure that the two people who are working it aren't pushing it to make those words?" I asked.

"Well, if they're dumb enough to want to kid themselves—that's up to them," he said.

"Well, did it work the time you watched it?" I asked.

"It was spooky. It was very spooky," he said. "There were two artists and a writer there, and myself. And a couple of other people. Apparently messages did come through."

"*You* were playing with a Ouija board, John?" I asked. "Want to clarify what 'came through' is supposed to mean? It's so vague a term."

"I get the message, Elizabeth," he said. "I was just taking down the letters they called out."

"Fuller—the journalist—playing with a Ouija board? And all this time, I thought you were so much into facts."

"No, I wasn't playing with it," he insisted. "I was just taking down the messages that came over."

"Well, could we try it?"

"Do you know how ridiculous that would sound in a factual book?" he said.

"What's the difference between Ouija boards and ghosts?" I asked.

"I think we have a lot more digging to do before we go out and buy any Ouija boards," he said. "Remember that stewardess? The one who reported seeing the apparition of Don Repo? She said it actually formed in front of her. She was in the lower galley of the L-1011."

"Yes. Wasn't that Ginny Packard*?" I asked.

"Right. I want to follow up my first interview with her. And your presence will help. She can relate to you as a stewardess," he said.

I agreed. It would be good to get back to straight, down-to-earth interviews again.

In spite of the intensive course at the school, my life didn't change drastically, as John had feared. But I did learn how to reach out and unlock a few psychic doors, doors I had never dreamed about before. I had discovered a metaphysical key, but the haunting questions now were: Would this key unlatch the psychic doors leading to clues of Don Repo? Could I receive any new insight into his mysterious appearances? More important, and crazy as the idea was, would I be able to receive any *direct* messages that would confirm the reality of the Ghost of Flight 401?

I was anxious to look for these answers. John wasn't so anxious. We had our priorities. Our first priority was to check as many firsthand witnesses as

---

Elizabeth Fuller

possible. It was important to make sure we had a case, a strong case. Then we could begin our own search.

At this point, John had still been pushing hard with his interviews. By the time my course had finished, he had chalked up a considerable number of long, intensive interviews with Eastern pilots, stewardesses, ramp agents, and mechanics. In addition to that, there were at least a dozen or so pages of transcripts, plus several notebooks crammed with handwritten notes.

The interviews and other material had one common denominator: over a period of many months Don Repo was reported to be seen on the L-1011s. Recently, however, the reports had died off. I wondered: Could the "soul rescues" have anything to do with the drop-off?

John had been successful in setting up a meeting with the Packards. Ginny was on a day off, and we were invited to visit with them in their Fort Lauderdale home, that same evening.

It was a typical low-slung Florida ranch-style house. It looked a little like a compact version of Arthur Ford's sprawled-out home in South Miami. The interior was light and airy. The furniture was mostly of white wicker. Hanging everywhere were huge pots of Boston ferns.

Fred* answered the door. He was somewhere in his late thirties. I could sense that he wasn't ecstatic over our visit. At first, he seemed rather circumspect. He was cordial, but distant. I really couldn't blame the guy. I probably would have been equally suspicious, given the same circumstances.

I felt as if Fred were just being protective of his wife. He, too, worked for an airline. I'm sure he was well aware of how airlines didn't take to unconventional behavior, ghosts included. However, John and I did our best to persuade them gently that their identity would be kept top secret. John shared some of his other research material with Fred. I think that helped him to feel more reassured about his wife's experience. We both told Fred about the dozens of other crew members who had reported a similar type of experience.

John had always found that in any research it is best to share what you know first. Especially, in a case as bizarre as this one. People felt uncomfortable when dealing with a subject matter that went beyond the norm.

Ginny broke the ice when she joined us in their screened-in patio. She was tall, slim, lively, and enthusiastic. John had been introduced to Ginny through Emily Palmer,* another Eastern flight attendant.

John had first met Emily on a flight from New York to Miami. He loved the L-1011s, and felt they were the best planes in the air, ghost or no ghost. In the process of canvasing the crew members, John was fortunate enough to run into Emily. Emily told John that not only had she heard of the stories, but had actually collected over two dozen different accounts. It had become a hobby with her. The accounts of the apparitions had intrigued her to the point of diligently recording long case histories of where, when, who, and how. Some of her reports, she said, were gathered from crew members who had direct contact with the ghost. Her stories included everything from cold, clammy feelings to full-bodied apparitions.

Emily told John that she felt certain that there

was some truth behind her personal ghost-log. She didn't see any reason why crew members would want to make up something as ridiculous as this. Although Emily said she had never had any ghostly encounters herself, some of her colleagues had. One of them turned out to be Ginny Packard.

Ginny, in turn, had put John in touch with two other Eastern stewardesses. John said it was that way all along with his interviews. One led to another, down the line. All three of them had met John during a preliminary interview. All three of them had experienced the ghost, in one way or another.

Fred Packard was an executive with another airline. He didn't hesitate to tell us that he was skeptical of the paranormal. But he also went on to say that in spite of his skepticism, he believed his wife completely.

"Ginny," he said, "isn't prone to any sort of exaggerations. In fact, she has never talked about anything that could be considered psychic before. Neither one of us put much faith into that area. I still don't," he said. "All I know is that Ginny was really shook up over what she had seen.

"I never saw anybody in such a state," he continued. "When she came home it was as if she had seen a ghost." We all laughed. Ginny could now joke about it. She was no longer frightened. It was just the initial shock, she said—the unexpectedness.

Ginny told us that now she intentionally tried to fly the L-1011, ship 318, just in case the amorphous flight engineer decided to drop by for another visit. She said, "A lot of stews are afraid of it, but there's a lot more that bid for Flight 401. Just because of the ghost."

Before John and I had gone over to the Packards', John had told me of his lengthy interview with Ginny and the other two Eastern stews. It was the first time I had heard her story, but John had specifically wanted Ginny to go over it again. He wanted to compare the two versions, he told me later.

"It was a night flight," she began. "I was down in the lower galley all alone. It was ship 318. I was standing there waiting for someone to send the lift down from above. It must have taken five minutes."

Ginny swung both of her legs off the floor and onto the sofa. Then she asked:

"Elizabeth, have you seen an L-1011 galley?"

I nodded. I thought back to the time I visited one. John had asked me to try to visit an L-1011 galley to get a description of it. It was before he had a chance to check it out himself. One of my friends was an Eastern ramp agent. He gave me a guided tour of the spacious lower bay. To get down into it, there are two skinny elevators, big enough for either two bony stewardesses or one stewardess and a service cart. The galley looked like something out of a science-fiction flick set in the year 2000. It was bright, shiny stainless steel, with enough ovens to cook up to two hundred meals. Strangely enough, it wasn't the least bit spooky down there. The antiseptic kitchen seemed like such an unlikely haunt for a ghost. While Ginny was telling us of her experience, I felt as if I were standing in the lower galley with her.

She continued: "The elevators still hadn't come. I just happened to look off to my right. There's a storage area that leads off from the galley to the electrical power section.

"Then I saw a cloudy, hazy type of thing over by

the electrical door." Ginny stopped her story as she picked up her toy poodle and sat him on her lap.

"I was still waiting for one of the elevators. I looked over my shoulder again. The cloudy formation was still there. But it was becoming more solid. It was not condensation or smoke. To make sure, I checked a nearby vent. I kept pushing the elevator button. It still didn't come. I was curious as to what that hazy, cloudlike thing was. But at the same time, I didn't want to know."

I felt what Ginny was saying. My heart was pounding as if it were happening to me. I could identify with her. She never had anything paranormal happen to her before, either.

"I forced myself to glance over again," Ginny went on. "This hazy thing was now much more solid. It was about a foot in diameter. It began to pulsate. Gradually, it took on a distinct shape. I couldn't take my eyes off it. As I continued to watch, it began to form into the shape of a face. I looked away for what seemed like minutes, but was probably only seconds. When I looked back it was clearly the shape of a man's face, complete with hairline and glasses. Just then the elevator came. I got the hell out of there."

It was hard for me to conceive of a ghost as something other than a white sheet over a prankster's head. But John told me about a scientist he had been studying, named G.N.M. Tyrell. He was also a famous investigator for the British Society of Psychical Research. In addition, to being a scientist, he was a pioneer in the development of the radio, an engineer and a mathematician. He had devoted forty years to psychical research.

Tyrell did not agree with the commonly held notion of white sheets over heads. He found too much evidence that pointed in another direction. Through thousands of case studies of individuals who claimed to have seen a ghost or apparition, he compiled a series of characteristics of what a ghost was supposed to look like.

He found in his studies that they often appear real and solid, to the extent that details like color and texture of skin and clothing were no different from those of a real person. You could walk around the apparition and see every detail. If you turned on the light, you could see it better; it wouldn't fade.

If it were wearing a rose, you might even smell it. You might hear it breathing, hear its footsteps, and notice that it blocks out the background behind it. If it were in front of a mirror, you could see its reflection. If you closed your eyes, it would disappear, but the chances are it would still be there when you opened them again.

Although Ginny encountered a more hazy, misty type of apparition, many of Eastern's crew members reported seeing Don Repo as a solid full-bodied apparition. One of the reports in John's notebook read:

> Flight engineer came to the flight deck before doing "walk around" preflight inspection and engineering panel check . . . Saw man in Eastern's second officer uniform sitting in his seat at the panel . . . The engineer quickly recognized him as Don Repo . . . The apparition of Repo said something like: "You don't need to worry about the preflight, I've already done it." . . . Almost immediately the three-dimensional image of Repo disappeared, vanished . . .

Probably, the most dramatic and most consistent of all the reports was the "Mexico City Incident." This had been written up in the Flight Safety Foundation Bulletin. It was also one of my early barf-bag reports.

Repo had appeared to two stewardesses and a flight engineer in the lower galley. He spoke audibly. He told them to watch out for a fire on the plane. He then disappeared. Later there was a fire. However, the captain was able to land the L-1011 on just one engine.

John and I were in the process of tracking down some direct sources on this New York–Mexico City run. Again, it would be difficult. Again, we would be surprised.

What bothered John so much was that it was so difficult to get people to talk. As a crew member myself, I understood their position. They were afraid of ridicule and equally afraid of being sent to the company shrink.

Ginny's story, compounded with those of the Chamberses, Manning, Laura, Emily's notes, going over the results of John's interviews, plus my own experiences, convinced me that there was a strong case for the Ghost of 401. I could even tell that John was slowly changing the course of his research. He was no longer just tracing how a jet-age legend might have been started. He was beginning to investigate a story that seemed to show evidence for survival after death.

Once again I brought up the Ouija-board idea. I suggested to John that we could experiment in between the interview type of research that he favored so strongly. After my irrational explanation of why we should try psychic exploration, he finally acquiesced. We would begin to try my idea on my next series of days off.

It was at this point that our story began to turn. Neither John nor I ever expected to receive any unconventional direct information. If John would have known at that time how far "my idea" would lead us, I don't think he would have ever agreed to this sort of ethereal search. But we didn't know. Even I never dreamed of the possibility of receiving strange telegraphic messages coming from a 12" x 14" slab of wood. Soon the problem facing both of us would be: Would we get too submerged in this psychic pool to still tread water?

The story also began to turn in another way. It had nothing to do with Don Repo, airlines, or ghosts. But it was equally unexpected.

CHAPTER IX

WITH THE COURSE completed and my brief furlough over, it was time to leave Miami and go back to my "other life," as a stewardess. It was also time for me to drag out that red regulation cloth they call a uniform. For the next ten days, I would put "007" in cold storage and replace it with 1016, my airline seniority number.

I was ambivalent about leaving Miami, and those fantastic experiences. I was hoping that once I was out of that heavy psychic scene, I wouldn't lose what I had learned. I was also sad to leave behind a writer who was growing more irascible every day over the ghost story.

I would be flying a seven-day trip, originating in Minneapolis. Our first layover point was Los Angeles. From there, we flew to Honolulu for a layover, then on to Tokyo, where we would spend a night and a day. Then the whole thing would be reversed, finally ending up back in Minneapolis one week, 25,000 miles, and 3,800 passenger meals later. There were no tears when the crews would arrive back at home base. We must have walked half those miles on the 747 carpets.

But I was now in the middle of that back-breaking journey. We were only some 12,000 miles into our trip. We had just left Honolulu, and had passed over the long chain of islands that stretches westward from Hawaii. From 35,000 feet, in the fading light, they looked like a series of punctuation marks dotting the Pacific. Our passengers were sleeping off the free miniatures of assorted booze, and their dinners: a choice of Mahi-Mahi or Chicken Teriyaki, two fancy names for fish and fowl. I was exhausted.

There had been a two-hour ground delay leaving Honolulu. In cabin-attendant vernacular this simply meant: you offer free liquor until they drop. It's just a shifty little airline trick that seems never to fail at pacifying passengers, even though it turns your otherwise friendly cabin attendants into hostile miscreants.

I was back in my old think tank, a darkened 747 jump seat. I had a lot of things to think about. Ever since I had left John at Miami Airport, I had replayed hours of our dialogue on my mental Sony TC-55. I carefully reconstructed the visual images of John and myself over the recent past. After several days of this type of analysis, I summoned up a Great Truth: there actually hadn't been a great Moment of Truth. It was more like a series of minor events that continued to accumulate until they reached stark reality. For lack of better words—I was in love with the guy.

John and I were definitely not like any characters out of a Daphne du Maurier novel. It was much more serious than the rich English girl who found excitement, danger and passion as she dared to love a pirate, a devil-may-care adventurer.

Our scenario would be much more gripping: Girl from Ohio. She finds excitement, a little bit of dan-

ger (on an airboat trip), but no evident passion with
an annoying writer. An overly cautious one at that,
who has never more than hinted at his affections for
her. Together, they chase ghosts, get on each other's
nerves, and eventually live happily ever after in a
shack somewhere in Connecticut.

The truth of the matter was that real-life situations always continued past the happily-ever-after
stage. Nothing ever stayed the same, except when
you'd rather it changed.

I wondered what would happen to me if our
relationship evolved into more than just what it was
now. And I really had no idea what it was now.
Maybe I was in love with the idea of a writer, and a
rather adventurous writer at that. I've always ro-
manticized about such lives. I wondered what it
would be like when Fuller was working on one of
those dozen or more books he had written. He
already had told me that when he wrote he got up at
4:30, jogged, ate a big breakfast, and worked almost
straight through to 6 P.M. At that time, he said, he
would mix two hefty man-sized martinis, watch the
news, eat dinner, and collapse, as he re-read the
day's typed pages.

What if I would quit my job flying? Would John
expect me to hang around the hut? Type his manu-
scripts? Worse than that, clean his house? Now I had
the best of two worlds. With my job, I had the fringe
benefits that airlines offer, free passes to go anywhere at any time. I also had the mental stimulation
of Fuller, even though at times it was pure aggrava-
tion.

I remembered John saying that maybe my marriage hadn't worked out because I was always off
flying. That was a good hint that Fuller was probably the guy who expected his woman to stick around

the house and make real meals. Now that I thought about it, Fuller was sort of a chauvinist, but an innocuous one. He always carried my bags, opened doors for me, and made sure he walked nearer to the street.

There would be an opportunity to think all this over at closer range. John wanted to go over all the research material systematically with me, so that I could transcribe hours of taped interviews, catalogue the information, read and outline nearly two dozen journals on parapsychology. He wanted to dig deeper into academic studies on the theory of apparitions in search of evidence of the human consciousness surviving after death. I noticed that when Fuller researched, he researched.

In spite of John's chauvinism, and compulsion for research, I was looking forward to seeing him in Connecticut. It would also give me a chance to visit with some friends of mine who lived in nearby Ridgefield. I had five days I could spare to work on the research. And I still had that Ouija-board idea in the back of my mind.

John met me at La Guardia. I had offered to take the airport limousine out to Westport but he wouldn't hear of it. We pushed our way out of the knotted La Guardia traffic and soon were moving along the Merritt Parkway, where there were real, actual trees—all of them wearing snowsuits on this chilly winter day.

I had been to Connecticut once before, but it had been in the summer. Now it looked like a Currier & Ives Christmas card. We turned off the Merritt Parkway, onto the narrow side roads, back country from Westport. Rimming the roads were evergreens and pines and low stone walls. There was a thick blanket of snow on the ground. John pointed out several pre-Revolutionary War houses, with big, squat central chimneys. The white clapboards were sparkling in the bright winter sun.

I heard it here for the first time, as we drove past stone walls and a weathered barn. John actually said he missed me. I returned the compliment. There was a moment of silence. Then he just plain said: "I love you." Just like that. I tensed up, and didn't say anything. He glanced over at me for some sort of reaction. I said something real deep, like: Oh.

There was silence again. What else was there to say? I wanted to tell him, but I couldn't get it out. I felt as if I were back in high school. Now I was starting to wonder if I heard him properly. Maybe he had just said he loved Connecticut. I couldn't say "I love you," if I weren't sure he said he loved me. It could have been wishful thinking. Besides, several moments had elapsed since he said that, if that was what he said. I couldn't ask him to repeat it—or could I?

I could. He repeated it. This time I said it quick, without batting an eye: "Love you, too, Fuller." Again there was silence. Then he reached over, grabbed my hand, and squeezed it. In doing so, we almost spun out on an icy spot, coming uncomfortably close to one of those stone walls.

John's house was not exactly what I'd pictured. It was much better: a tiny green cottage on a white-water river, with Dickens-bookstore-type windows. The house definitely looked like Fuller. The inside was equally charming. John told me that he did all the interior paneling himself. None of the work looked really professional. Most of it was on angle. But the flaws just added to the overall effect—coziness and warmth.

His study was impressive. The room looked like

an illustrated biography. The paneling was pep-
pered with framed reminders of past books, documentary films and plays written or produced. Lined
up on the floor next to his desk were five huge
cartons of research material, and at least a dozen
textbooks on nuclear physics. They were for a book
he had just finished. It was about the dangers of
nuclear power plants. He told me that as hard as it
was to research that book, the ghost story was even
harder.

The place would never be spotless, but I hate
Clorox-clean houses. There were just enough cobwebs to make it believable. John was proud of how
he spent all day cleaning the place up. I was flat-
tered.

In the living room was a fireplace that was prepared to be lighted. John told me that he planned on
broiling some steaks to go along with a bottle of
Chateauneuf du Pape.

God, this whole thing was too much like a Holly-
wood script—girl falls in love with older writer—
they rendezvous at his little cottage—have candlelit
dinner with moderately expensive French wine—
discuss the next step in their research—then kiss.
And we did just that.

The next morning, John showed me portions of
some Stewart Edward White books he had been
researching. Stewart White, like John, had been a
journalist. He had written many well-known books,
one of them being *The Unobstructed Universe*. He
got involved in the psychic after playing with a
Ouija board with his wife, Betty. He had become
intrigued with the results of the Ouija board, not
because of any unusual messages, but rather because it had moved without any apparent conscious

activity on his part. Convinced that he was not moving the indicator (several times he had tried to guide it in a certain direction, and it had pulled away from him), he had then become certain that it was either his partner moving it or an unconscious muscular action.

White had been mildly amazed at receiving full sentences that were not on either his or his wife's mind. But he had been even more amazed at how the thing felt under his fingertips. White wrote that it had a certain life, a vitality about it. But he also acknowledged that it could have all been in his imagination.

White and his wife had then begun some experiments. It was not because they had wanted to receive any communications. They didn't even believe in that sort of thing. They had been curious as to how the thing moved, the phenomenon behind the motion.

The results of their experiments eventually led to his wife's psychic development. It also led to her recording three books of spiritual insight by auto-matic writing where the hand moves without conscious guidance. Automatic writing was simply one other form of psychic mediumship. White referred to her handwritten recordings as a view of the "unobstructed universe." Hence, the title of one of his books. It was a profound book, that apparently was dictated from the "other side." According to White, his wife was a channel.

John said that the book made him feel a little better about trying out a Ouija board. He sort of identified with the tough-minded journalist White—or at least that's what he muttered all the way to the store.

Before we even got out of the car, John handed me some money. He smiled and asked me if I would mind buying the board, while he picked up something in the hardware department. As soon as we got inside the glass door, John took off. I asked one of the salespeople if they could tell me where I could find a Ouija board. I was directed to the toy section. I was glad John didn't hear that.

As I was paying for it, I realized that I was a couple of dollars short. I yelled over to where John was fidgeting with some sort of appliance. He was practically at the opposite end of the store. "Hey, Fuller, I don't have enough money for the Ouija board!" I yelled. I'm glad he wasn't near any Saturday night specials at the time.

We got back to the house. John was surprisingly flexible. It must have been Stewart Edward White's experience combined with that session up at the New Hampshire writer's colony he had mentioned. John had told me that a verifiable message from the deceased poet, Eleanor Wylie, had "come through" over the board. This sounded sort of wild coming from John, but he meant it.

We sat down opposite each other. We rested the board on our knees, as per the instructions. We placed our fingertips lightly on the plastic indicator. In the center of the indicator was a little window. This was so you could see which letter it stopped on. Then, the spiderlike indicator began moving in a wide circle, as if someone were winding up an alarm clock. Then it slowed down, and stopped, before moving onto a long series of letters.

We could tell that the letters weren't making any sense. We finally realized that if the damn thing were going to work, we would need the assistance of the ever-faithful TC-55. We could then call out the letters, then transcribe whatever letters came over from the cassette.

We did this. We started calling letters out. The indicator definitely was moving, and not under my propulsion, at least. I accused John of moving it. He accused me of the same thing. We almost got into a fight. But when we transcribed the first long series of letters, there was nothing but gibberish. We took a rest and tried again.

This time I sensed something was happening. The letters came so fast we barely had time to call them out to the tape deck. John wrote about those first opening messages in his book, *The Ghost of Flight 401*. I quote his account of what happened because it was the beginning of something we never really expected:

> The letters were now being run off in a series, one after the other. But the problem was, they made no sense at all. We were calling out the letters on a tape recorder, and then played them back. They read:
>
> TGRATWEBYSWGRSNW
>
> "We're not reading you," Elizabeth said. "Will you try again?" Our instructions were to call out the questions vocally.
>
> TWAURVPTMITNXNY
>
> It made no sense whatever. There was no use of even trying to separate the letters. It was total gibberish.
>
> "We're not going to give up yet," Elizabeth said. "Keep going, whoever you are."

If the letters were meaningless, the movement of the indicator was still building up strength. It would swirl in a wide circle, as if it were generating energy, then move to letters and stop very clearly and deliberately.

TNGRDIOIOIO

Still nothing discernible. My back was tired and I was ready to quit. "Keep going, please," Elizabeth said to the board. Then, suddenly, the letters began to say something.

TWA KNOW REPO

I wondered immediately if this could be a random selection of letters. Julian Huxley had once postulated that if six monkeys sat at six typewriters, and banged away at random until infinity, they would eventually write all the classics of literature in correct order. Our letters could be complete coincidence.

"Who is here with us?" Elizabeth asked. "Spell the last name, please."

There was more unintelligible gibberish, which reinforced my theory that the one sequence that did make sense, was a random shot in the dark.

Then Elizabeth asked. "You mentioned 'Repo.' Is that correct?" The indicator swept up to YES and stopped. Then it went back to the letters and continued to spell. At each series, we would stop the tape recorder, write down the letters, and try to separate them into words.

GPNE TO TO UN POSNTN

It was not making any sense again. "Is this a place?" Elizabeth asked. The indicator slid quickly to YES again.

"On this earth?" Elizabeth said. Now the indicator shot to NO.

"Where?" she asked.

INFUTE INFINITE

It was getting more interesting. "What else can you tell us?" Elizabeth asked.

TWA 727 CHICAGO

Then the questions and answers came thick and fast:

"Are you a TWA crew member?"

YES

"Are you deceased?"

YES

"Were you killed in a crash?"

YES KNOW REPO

"What is your first name?"

DON

"Are we talking directly?"

NO

"Who are we talking through?"

TWA

"Do you have a message?"

YES

"Who is the message for?"

VNJOHN

"Last name, please."

FULLER

I was beginning to feel uncomfortable. All through this, I was watching Elizabeth's hands. Her fingers were still touching the indicator with the lightest of touches. I knew for certain I wasn't moving the indicator. I could constantly feel it pull away from me, so that I had to move my fingers to catch up with it at times. Elizabeth wanted to get on with the questioning. "What is the message?" she asked the board.

TO STOP WORRY

"Stop worrying about what?"

NAMES

In planning the writing of the book, I was constantly worried about the names of the people who had given me so much information. The last thing in the world I wanted was to put anybody in danger with his or her employer. Much of the material had been given to me in confidence. This was a real concern. But how did the inanimate Ouija board know this—or if it were Repo, how would he know it? And how would he know to come to the board, directly or indirectly? There would have to be a lot more confirmation for me to even begin to believe this.

"Is this really Don Repo on the board?" I asked.

YES

"Spell out your name, please."

DON REPO

"What kind of plane were you in in the crash?" I continued.

1011

This was interesting. I knew that the cabin crews referred to the plane as the L-1011, and that the cockpit crews used only the short form: 1011. I was determined to bear down hard.

"What was the plane number of the L-1011 that crashed?" I asked.

310

"Flight number?"

401

All this was correct. I was convinced by this time that neither Elizabeth nor I were consciously moving the indicator, that the instrument was spelling out articulate words that purported to be coming from Don Repo, and that much of the information was accurate. Just who the TWA crew member was, we would have to explore later. Further, I would have to get information that neither Elizabeth nor I knew anything whatever about, if we were to rule out our unconscious minds as the motivator of the messages on the board. Right at the moment, I wanted to get as much information as I could, as long as the letters were flowing freely.

It was difficult even when the letters did flow fast. They came as an unintelligible stream until we could divide them later.

We asked:

"What airline?"

EAL

This was the official designation for Eastern.

It was now time to get down to facts that the entity who identified himself as Repo would know, but which neither Elizabeth nor I did. At least the information we were getting was clear and correct. How we were getting it was a different matter. It seemed totally absurd that a toy could come up with information that could penetrate a wall between the known and the unknown. I was fully aware of how ridiculous this might appear in print, and torn about continuing with the device.

I recalled the words I had read of Professor Hyslop:

"The facts must prove that the source of the phenomena is what it claims to be, and this personal identity of the discarnate means that the deceased person shall tell facts of personal knowledge in his earthly life and tell them in such quantity and with such a quality that we should not doubt his existence any more than we would if we received the same incidents over a telegraph wire or through a telephone.

In this way alone can we show that the intelligence involved is outside the medium through which the facts come."

We had not reached that point yet, by any means. But it was impossible to resist going on.

Our romance almost came to an abrupt end during those early Ouija experiments. John absolutely refused to believe that I wasn't pushing that indicator. I crossed my heart. I made the girl scout's pledge. I said a few may-I-never-speak-another-word's. He still wouldn't believe me. It wasn't until I began accusing him of the same thing that he finally let up. I never before saw two such suspicious people. I began to watch him very closely. I couldn't be completely sure *he* wasn't moving it, but I could be sure of one thing: I was not consciously moving that indicator.

The logical explanation was that it was our unconscious that was doing the moving. It was unconscious muscular activity that had spelled out that information. But there was something that bothered me—why would my unconscious and John's unconscious agree on where to move the indicator? It would be a pretty far-out premise to think that there could have been any collusion between our two unconscious minds. But I suppose that is still not as strange as the alternative—spirit communication.

Whatever the phenomena behind that thing moving it was very strange. Was there an outside force pushing that indicator around to the various letters?

I was still getting used to the idea of a "Spiritual Society." That was hard enough to digest; now this.

We were both beginning to wonder if this ghost research could be killing off our brain cells. It was almost impossible to conceive of a force completely outside of us that was actually creating those answers.

During that first session we didn't receive any information that we didn't already know. This was certainly no test for "spirit communication." To be totally realistic, I had to examine all possibilities. Maybe I wanted this experiment to work so much that I unconsciously moved it to those letters. I doubted that, but I had to consider it as a real possibility. In our next session John and I would have to be careful to ask questions that we didn't know the answers to.

That afternoon, John and I decided to go to the library and see what we could find on the Ouija board. In our search we came across a very interesting case.

In 1912, a St. Louis housewife by the name of Mrs. Pearl Curran began experimenting with a Ouija board along with her friend, Mary Pollard. After a long series of garbled messages, a very unusual message spelled itself out:

OH WHY LET SORROW STEAL THY HEART THY BOSOM IS BUT ITS FOSTER MOTHER THE WORLD ITS CRADLE AND THE LOVING HOME ITS GRAVE

This language seemed to be from the 1600s. Neither of the women had ever written any poetry before. Neither had ever spoken such flowery language. They continued with their experiment and similar messages followed, all perfectly literate. The amazing thing was that neither woman had ever gone beyond elementary school. After continuous messages in the same style the "spirit" personality identified herself:

MANY MOONS AGO I LIVED AGAIN I COME PATIENCE WORTH MY NAME IF THOU SHALT LIVE THEN SO SHALL I MAKE MY BREAD AT THY HEARTH GOOD FRIENDS LET US BE MERRIE THE TIME FOR WORK IS PAST LET THE TABBY DROWSE AND BLINK HER WISDOM TO THE FIRELOG

Another message that came from the alleged Patience Worth suggested that maybe we all doubt strange, unknown phenomena too much:

AH CLIMB NOT THE STAIRS TO FIND A PEBBLE WHY STRIP THE ROSE THE SCENT IS THINE WITHOUT THE WASTE O HELL ITSELF IS BUT A HOME FOR DOUBTERS

The messages were eventually turned into complete novels. The sessions lasted for several years and totaled over a million words. There never has been an adequate explanation.

The Ouija board alone would never have startled me. It was this, combined with all those other "communications" I had received. The night at that séance. Those five readings in class. And now this crazy board. As difficult as it was for me to accept, maybe I really was a channel for the "other side"?

I thought back to the question that I had asked myself on the night before my course. If by some quirk of nature I ever developed into a medium, could *I* possibly solve this ghost story? If there was this ghost, Don Repo, and he really was communicating with those Eastern employees, then why couldn't he communicate with me?

Maybe now I would start to get some answers.

I think John's belief system was a little bit rattled after that first Ouija-board session. While I was in the study transcribing and rechecking the tape recording of the Ouija-board sequences up to that time, I could hear John in the next room. He was talking to somebody about the Ouija board. I'm sure it wasn't his editor.

Later he came into the office and told me that he needed some reassurance that it was okay to go ahead with our experiments. So he had phoned the pilots in New York.

Both of the pilots had given John the same advice. They said that although it is possible to get accurate, clear messages, it is equally possible to get impostors. I thought that sounded awfully weird. John went on to say that according to the pilots, the best way to avoid receiving false information is to constantly cross-check everything that comes through. In other words, if it were a phony, we could trip the sucker up.

John later put a footnote in his "401" book strictly warning against the frivolous use of the board. It read: "Serious students of parapsychology emphatically warn against the use of the Ouija board for any prolonged time, or for frivolous attempts at communicating with purported 'spirits.' The phenomenon of possession, they say, is not to be taken lightly, and beyond that, the inclination to utilize the device as a crutch or support for decisions that should be made by the individual's free will, could grow to a point where serious psychological damage could result. As a device for guidance and forecasting of future, it could be totally unreliable. Specific case histories show that some people, just as in alcoholism, form a psychological dependency, and can be particularly vulnerable to the device."

I thought back to when I was a child. My brother and I used to drag out the Monopoly game. We would play for hours on end. During that time, the miniature plastic houses and hotels all came alive. My toy money was as real to me as my allowance. But the game ended. I was no longer a rich entrepreneur. As all kids, I could slip in and out of fantasy twenty-five times a day.

The Ouija board we were using came in the same type of box as that Monopoly game. It had directions that were written in a very serious tone, just as the Monopoly game had. The first time John and I tried the Ouija board, I had slipped back into an ultra-real world. A world like the one that contained Boardwalk, Park Place, and Baltic Avenue. The only difference was that this time, after we left the Ouija board, that ultra-real world gave evidence of existing.

John came into the office where I was finishing up the typing. He said he was ready for our next Ouija session anytime I was. I immediately packed up the transcribing, and followed him into the living room.

I couldn't believe my eyes. It was in the middle of the day, but the place looked like a morgue. The shutters and draperies were all pulled tight. It took me a few seconds to realize that John was really paranoid about experimenting with the board. He said that he didn't want to take any chances on having anybody just drop by. And that we were too close to the road; that cars might see in. I seriously doubted that anybody would peer in the windows, or that cars would slow down for a better look. But if it made him feel better, I wouldn't argue. I was just glad he was going along with the idea.

This time there were no accusatory remarks on either part. The next series of messages are a composite of the five days I was in Connecticut. Each letter was called out, as the indicator stopped. Each letter, whether it seemed to make sense or not, was recorded on the tape cassette. Half the time it seemed to be gibberish. A lot of the time, the sentences only made partial sense. But out of all this came a sense of truth, a sense of validity, that neither of us could deny. This guy, Repo, was emerging as *real*. I couldn't explain it. John couldn't explain it. But here was a personality sending us clear and sometimes garbled Western Union telegrams that were fascinating:

Q. What was the basic cause of the crash?
A. NOSE GEAR

Q. Can you give us more information?
A. THE PILOT EVERGLADES FRIEND HAD MORE HURT FOR US PILOTS IN EASTERN CREW IN THEIR HOUSE THE GIRLS SEE ME IN GALLEY OVEN DID MICE LEAVE THAT FAMILY CLOSET

Q. Were you clearly seen by crew members and passengers when you reappeared on the L-1011s?
A. SOME DID SOME DID NOT

Q. Did you appear before crew members who knew you before the accident?
A. USUALLY

Q. Can you give us your wife's first name?
A. SASSY

Q. Maybe it was a nickname?
A. NO

Q. What is the correct name?
A. ANICE

Q. Spell that again, please.
A. ALICE

Q. Can you give us the name of one of your daughters?
A. DONNA

Q. Can you give us the first name of one of your sisters?
A. MARY ANN

Q. Can you name the two others?
A. SEE NEWS CLIP IN YOUR HAND

Q. Have you got any general messages for us?
A. TO GO PHONE DONNA

Q. Do you have any messages for Donna, if we should call her?
A. FORGET DAD JOHN TO PHONE HER TELL HER I AM FINE WORKING HARD

169

Q. Any other messages for her?
A. BE GOOD GIRL   PS I LOVE HER VERY MUCH

Q. Are there any messages for your wife Alice, Don?
A. I LOVE HER FORGET DON TEARS DONT HELP ME TO COME BACK

Q. Don, name three things you check on a preflight walk-around.
A. WHEELS   VISUAL NOSE GEAR   TIRES

Q. Anything else you can tell us?
A. TO GO INTO WASTE BASKET PENNIES SIT THERE BOYS' ROOM

Q. Anything else, Don?
A. TO GO TO WORK ON STORY TELEPHONE DONNA TODAY GO BACK TO WORK STORY MUST BE WRITTEN YOU ARE WASTING THE WHOLE STORY TO GO TO WORK SO GO TO TYPEWRITER YOU SEE CALL DONNA DO NOT USE WIJI BOARD ANY MORE TODAY GET ON STORY SEE YOU TOMORROW REPO GOODBYE

For the first time in the course of our research John was actually beginning to believe that maybe this ghost story was really true. The way those messages were communicated were indicative of some sort of separate personality. It was almost as if there were somebody standing over our shoulders.

The message that really startled us was: SEE NEWS CLIP IN YOUR HAND. John *had* a news clipping in his hand, with the names of the Repo family members.

Mary and Ann were two of his sisters. We were expecting it to spell out the other two sisters' names. Instead, the pointer went completely where we didn't expect it. We couldn't even follow what the letters spelled in that sentence, until I transcribed them from the tape. Whatever it was at the board, it definitely was beginning to show a sense of humor.

Alice was Don's wife. Donna was his daughter. She was a flight attendant for Eastern. This was still information that we knew. But the name Sassy was not in that clipping. He repeated Sassy several times during the sessions. We would learn more about Sassy later.

John was bothered about the constant message: CALL DONNA. He didn't want a personal involvement. It would be too difficult and awkward. There would be no graceful way to tell a family about our experiments. Besides, John had learned that other journalists had tried to call the family, and they would talk to no one.

I thought back to what Laura had told us early on in the research. She said that in her meditations, Don Repo kept "coming through" with messages to call his family. He also seemed adamant about wanting John to write the story. These messages that John had pooh-poohed, we were now receiving ourselves.

I also thought back to that first reading I had given at the school. Douglas, the man who had been killed in a car crash, had apparently come through during that reading. He, too, was adamant about wanting his sister and mother to know that he was not really dead; that he was alive; but in another realm.

This whole thing was so strange. The messages from the board were even more strange than those readings. This was probably because I have always thought of the Ouija boards in terms of a toy. I could tell that John was growing more concerned over the messages reading: CALL DONNA. He was facing two nagging questions: should he just ignore this possible communication? Or should he write to Donna in spite of his better judgment? It would be a tough decision.

In the interim, John and I were trying to figure out what Don meant by telling us to look for the pennies. It was ridiculous. Two allegedly grown adults looking all over for nonexistent copper pennies as the result of a Telex-type message from a Ouija board! The next step would have to be the Laughing Academy. Neither one of us knew what TO GO INTO WASTE BASKET PENNIES SIT THERE BOYS ROOM meant. I went into the two tiny bedrooms upstairs. I thought maybe he meant where John's son stayed when he slept over. But there were no pennies in any basket. I never expected to find any, of course. MICE IN THE FAMILY CLOSET was another enigma. Neither of us had ever heard of, nor used, the term "family closet."

I transcribed the rest of the messages off the Sony tapes. John and I sat down and studied them carefully. Most of the messages made sense. But PENNIES IN BOYS ROOM, SASSY, and MICE IN FAMILY CLOSET made no sense at all. All these, however, would pop up again in a most unexpected way.

Before I left to return to Minneapolis, John finally came to a decision. He would write Donna. He felt compelled to whether he wanted to or not. Since we didn't have her address, we phoned Ginny Packard and she looked it up in the Miami directory.

John handled the letter with exceptional tact. He explained to Donna that he was not writing a disaster story. He also made it clear that in no way would his book reflect badly on any of the crew members or Eastern Airlines, which was absolutely true. He especially stressed that the theme of the book would be one of hope, and the possibility of life after death. John also mentioned in his letter that I was his research assistant, and that I, also, was a cabin attendant. He wrote that during the course of our research we had run into many accounts of her father's reappearances on the L-1011. However, John did not mention anything about our own experiments. He closed the letter by inviting Donna and her mother to join us in Miami for dinner.

John was a nervous wreck after writing that letter. He had sacrificed his entire belief system on an impulse. I was frankly shocked that he actually wrote it. I didn't know at that time if he had made the right choice or not. We were both too close and maybe a little emotional over those communications. Now, we would just have to wait it out.

After we mailed the letter off, John and I returned to the Ouija board. We were both determined to try to get some evidential information. As the session turned out we did get some information. Don Repo was a character.

Q. What state were you from before you came to Florida?

A. NEW YORK TEXAS KANSAS ISLAND MAINE CALIFORNIA BOSTON ATLANTA GEORGIA HARD TO VERIFY

Q. Please be serious, Don.

A. SEE ST. LOUIS INSTEAD SOUTH CAROLINA
WAS LOUISIANA SOMETIMES

(Later, we found that Don had been based in all these places in the Air Force.)

Q. Why do you do this, Don?
A. FUN TO GAG WITH YOU

Q. What are the main sections of the plane you appeared in?
A. COACH CLASS GALLEY OVEN

Q. What are your reasons for coming back, Don?
A. TO PLAY GAMES TODAY

Q. Be serious, Don.
A. DON LIKES TO CLOWN AROUND AND GAG HERE IN SPIRIT YOU SEE I LIKE TO JOKE AROUND

It's impossible to describe the feelings of a personal touch we got from these sentences. We would actually *feel* Don's presence—not in any sepulchral way, but in a sense of buoyancy and lightheartedness that seemed to take away the sting of death more than a dozen convivial wakes. This man was real, and he was lovable.

Then, for no logical reason I could think of, I asked a ridiculous question:

Q. Don, can you tell us something to prove that you're really here?
A. GOLD RING WILL BREAK

I was wearing a gold ring. I took it off and we examined it. It certainly didn't look as if it would break. It was less than five years old. John didn't wear any jewelry. With that message we decided to knock off the Ouija session. From the looks of those messages, John felt even worse about mailing that letter off to Donna, but it was too late to worry about that now.

We decided to forget about research temporarily. For my last night in Connecticut, we would go out and have a good dinner.

John took me to Pierre's, a quietly elegant French restaurant in Westport. We ordered coq au vin, and another bottle of Chateauneuf du Pape.

Again the scene was romantic, and being romantic, it brought me back to the condition in which we found ourselves: in love.

We had never mentioned anything about an exclusive relationship. It was too new. It didn't seem necessary. But I was still curious as to what John would be up to while I was on my trip. So I asked him. He was a little bit short of annoyingly coy. He just said, "What do you think?"

"Whip up new eggplant recipes, and blast Alice Cooper albums?"

"You're close," he said. "I'm going to clean up the house. Even better than it was this time."

"Well, what about when you finish cleaning up the hut?"

"Wait a minute," he said. "You're the one who's going to all those faraway, exotic places."

"They're not that exciting, and you of all people would know it," I said. "Once you've seen Tokyo, the thrill is gone. I might as well be back in Cleveland."

175

"You're sure?" John said, as if he didn't believe me.

"Well, maybe not Cleveland." We both laughed. For some reason, I just knew what John's next question was going to be. I was right. He asked me if the age difference bothered me. I told him that it didn't bother me, as much as it bothered him.

"How do you know that it bothers me?" he asked.

"Simple, remember when we were talking about the gurus?"

"Yes," he said. "Down in Miami."

"Well, remember when you said something about you couldn't fall in love with a female guru because she'd probably be too young for you?"

"You've got a good memory," he said.

"Fuller, was *I* that female guru?"

"Are you sure you're not a detective?"

I told John that I didn't care about things like that. Chronological years are just numbers that inhibit you from really living. Society is a real drag, the way it dictates that at a certain age you get married, you retire, you go to an old folks home, and then you die. And we, like fools, try our damndest not to let society down. We live up to those idiotic standards, I told him.

"You're too idealistic, Liz."

"I'm too much of a realist to be idealistic. I realize that I'm in love with you. I don't give a damn if we grow old gracefully or ungracefully together. If I wanted somebody my own age, and with my same interests, I would go to Computer Dating."

Over coffee, we got down to the serious business of what we were going to do next. Everything now seemed to hinge on the letter to Donna Repo. Without some kind of verification of the strange messages that had come over the board, they would be useless, and our serious inquiry into the rational possibility of an afterlife would remain unanswered.

I cannot ask anyone to really believe some of the things that were to follow. They're out of the realm of believability. The only thing I can say in my defense is that I'm physically strong, mentally awake, and morally straight, as the Boy Scouts put it. John will back me up on these strange events. But his rule during the writing of the *Flight 401* book was not to print anything of a subjective nature, or anything that couldn't be confirmed by outside sources. Therefore, he didn't mention any of these incidents in his book. My rule during the writing of *this* book is to print everything that happened, exactly as it happened.

CHAPTER X

I PHONED JOHN from Honolulu. I couldn't stand the suspense of waiting for that letter. He told me that he had heard from Donna, but he said it was too complicated to explain over the phone. He would tell me the whole story in three days, when I was back in Connecticut. I knew that it must have been good news. He didn't sound like a prophet of doom.

John picked me up at La Guardia. He waited until we got back to his house before telling me the upshot of that letter.

The letter we first mailed off to Donna had been returned. It was stamped: NO SUCH ADDRESS. At that point, John told me, it looked like a lost cause. But on another impulse, he phoned Ginny and asked her if she would mind seeing if the Miami phone directory had a listing for Alice Repo. It did. So John had mailed the same letter off to Donna, but in care of her mother. That way, John said, if Donna thought that it would upset her mother, she didn't have to show it to her. John didn't know what to expect. He prepared himself for the worst. Then, he said, four days later, the phone rang. It was Donna.

She told John that something very strange had just happened. She had just returned from a trip. Her mother dropped by to visit, and brought along

John's letter. After her mother left, Donna read the
letter. She was about to rip it up, when the phone
rang. It was her mother. She asked Donna what was
the name of the person in the return address on the
envelope. Donna told her that it was John G. Fuller.
Her mother said that all the way home she had been
trying to figure out why that name sounded so fa-
miliar. When she got back home she suddenly realized why. A friend of hers had recently dropped off a
book for her to read. Alice had stayed up half the
night reading it. She thought it was one of the most
absorbing books she had ever read. It was *Arigo:
Surgeon of the Rusty Knife*. It was a book John had
written several years earlier. Alice then told Donna
that in spite of their policy not to talk to journalists,
they wanted to meet us. There were delays and
postponements. The schedules of John, Donna, and
me were difficult to mesh. The dinner was finally set
for March 7 at the Marriott in Miami.

"Fuller," I said, "do you have any idea what that
means?"

"Yes. We're damn lucky."

"It's not us," I protested. "There's a very remote
chance it might be Don Repo. Suppose he's arranged this whole thing? You don't know. It might
even be a cosmic signal."

"Liz, take it easy."

"I can't take it easy. What do you need to make
you believe that there's something out there?"

"I admit that it's a very strange coincidence."

"A coincidence? Fuller, if your book hadn't been
given to Mrs. Repo, then Donna would have never
phoned you in a million years."

He said, "I have to admit that this is very
strange."

"Hooray for Fuller. He has finally admitted to something."

"Liz. I have to admit to something else, too." He had a very serious look on his face.

"What's that?" I said.

"I didn't spend my entire time cleaning the house."

Then he handed me an envelope, and he walked into his office. I felt my heart get real heavy. I thought maybe he was going to break something to me. But nobody in real-life situations ever writes "Dear John" letters anymore. Maybe it was my two weeks' notice. I opened the envelope and read:

FOR ELIZABETH

In you I find the meeting place of love
With all its sweetness amplified, enlarged,
As if a cosmic battery were charged
With some rare energy we know not of.
The night assumes a buoyancy that lifts
Its darkness and its fitful shroud of gloom.
A bright, melodic lustre fills the room
That finds you there, a product of your gifts
That burn the darkness out of night. And yet
When you are gone, night's mantle will descend;
This tattered cloak, that once had sapphires set
In place of stars, will slump in sad regret,
No shred of incandescence there to mend
The pain—which only your return will end.

I was never good at emotional responses. I read it again. For some inexplicable reason, the poem evoked memories of my grandmother. I called her Old Ma. We were very close. She had a knack for taking even the most solemn of circumstances and pointing out the humor in it. She helped to make tolerable the crises of my teenage years. There was not one time we were ever together that we failed to have a good laugh.

Old Ma's motto was that if you can't laugh, you may as well lie down and die. In all those years we were together I never once told her I loved her. It was there, but unexpressed. Now, it was too late. So many times I wish I could have shouted up to the heavens: *Old Ma, I love you—I love you, Old Ma.* That one word was always so difficult for me to get out. I had the same feeling at this time.

John was coming out of his office. This time, I wouldn't let the moment go by.

"Fuller, you're not the klutz I thought you were," I said.

John wrapped his arms around me, as if he understood. Then we laughed. Maybe those words I had been unable to say weren't necessary, after all.

With the meeting with Donna and Mrs. Repo set up, the story was now assuming a poignancy we had never expected.

If these communications were true, and I strongly suspected that they were, then there must be some sort of life after death. I thought about the Kübler-Ross and Ritchie experiences again. Six months before, I would have shrugged their accounts of life after death off as subjective or just wishful thinking. Now, here I was with equally offbeat experiences. I was frustrated. I now believed in this sixth sense, or this Spiritual Society, or whatever label you wanted to give it, but even with this belief, I wanted to grab on to it, hold it down, examine it in the clear light of day. Maybe I was being outer-directed, but I still wanted to show John that something was happening.

Who would ever really believe these communications? Several months earlier, I certainly wouldn't have believed anyone who told me that this sort of thing had happened to him. How could I ever expect anyone to believe me? If John and I decided to follow Don's purported advice, and tell Donna and Alice of his messages, would they believe us? Would they think that this was all just a tasteless joke? There were a lot of questions. There were no apparent answers that would satisfy us.

The awesomeness of the very possibility of being in communication with someone who had died was enough to label us lunatics. And yet we were getting coherent and articulate messages from this ethereal Western Union in the sky.

I asked John if we could go back to the Ouija board again, and ask Don what he thought about us going down to Miami. From the messages, it was almost as if some Celestial Department of Engineering arranged for this dinner with Alice and Donna:

Q. You here, Don?
A. YES

Q. So you know what happened?
A. CALL FROM DONNA

Q. How did you feel about it?
A. ELATED HER FATHER BE NICE TO BABY GIRL
   FOR THE VISIT MRS KNOW I LOVE THEM

Q. What are we planning to do when we meet them?
A. TAKE TO DINNER

Q. How did you know that, Don?
A. SEE DON IS SMART

Q. I see you still have your sense of humor.
A. YES MRS MAKE HER JUST HAPPY HI FROM DON GOODBYE

We had found when the words GOODBYE were spelled, they meant just that. The indicator would all of a sudden just stop. For that reason alone, I felt as if those messages weren't coming from our unconscious. If they were, then we could have kept up the charade, and continued to fool ourselves. It certainly seemed as if somebody from beyond that board were running the show. We felt so helpless, so out of control. On the other hand, as crazy as it may sound, the words that had just come through were so warm and touching, we were beginning to love this shadowy person.

That night, as John and I were having dinner, we discussed the messages that we had received earlier. John kept arguing that all the incidents involving the Repos could be pure coincidence: the missent letter that eventually prevented it being thrown away; the receipt of his book by Mrs. Repo. My argument was that at some point, coincidences cease to be coincidences. And this was one of those times. Every once in a while, Fuller could be so thick he drove me crazy.

In between our rather heated discussions, we ate the Stouffer's frozen lasagne I had whipped up. I was about to take my last bite. The fork was halfway to my mouth. There was a sudden pinch on my finger. I said the expected: *Ouch!* John asked me what had happened. I put down the fork and examined my pinched finger. It was my ring finger.

My gold ring had snapped in two. I thought that was awfully strange. I hadn't bumped it. There didn't seem to be any apparent reason for the crack down the back of it. I handed it over to John. He, too, inspected the jagged piece of gold. He shrugged his shoulders and handed it back to me.

I got up from the table and was headed into the other room. I was going to put it in my handbag so I wouldn't lose it. I was just about to slip it into the zippered pocket of my purse when it suddenly struck me. That was the message from Don Repo several weeks earlier. At least, if my memory was correct. I dug out the Ouija board transcripts. It was *there*.

Q. Don, can you tell us something to prove that you're really here?
A. GOLD RING WILL BREAK ...

"Well, Fuller, what do you think now?" I asked.

"I think that's very strange. But it could still be a coincidence."

"I can't believe you," I said. "What does it take to make you believe?"

"I believe that it happened. I saw it. But we can't jump to conclusions," he said.

"Who's jumping to conclusions?"

"You are," he said.

"Fuller, you are actually bending over backward not to believe that things are happening," I said.

"No, Liz, that's not the case," he said. "We just have to be careful. It's too easy to be self-deluded."

"But you were working the Ouija board with me when we asked Don if he could tell us something to prove to us that he was really here," I said. "And then two weeks later, it happened. So why won't you accept it?"

"It's too subjective," he said.

"Of course, it's subjective. But it still happened."

I was furious with Fuller. Everything connected with this story was either strange, subjective, or a coincidence. He would admit to nothing else.

I was now determined to get to the bottom of this. I asked John if he would try the Ouija board with me again. I said if something else happened would he believe it then? He finally said he would try the board, but he made no other commitment. We sat down again, the board across our laps.

Q. Can you give us further proof?
A. READ NY TIMES PENNY WILL FIND THERE

Q. Who should read *Times*?
A. ELIZABETH

I was thinking that this guy really had a thing about pennies. He had given us a message once before: TO GO INTO WASTE BASKET PENNIES SIT THERE BOYS ROOM. That message meant nothing to us.

Q. Don, you know I won't find a penny. Why do you do that?
A. FUNNY GIRL

Q. But why do you play so many tricks?
A. FUN TO GAG

186

Q. Can you really do something to let us know you're here?

A. VISIT FLORIDA GO TO WORK STORY BYE

I went to the other room to get the *New York Times*. After my gold ring breaking, and regardless of the absence of pennies in the room John's son slept in, I was not going to ignore that message. I closely scanned every page of the *Times*. There was no penny to be found anywhere.

John was infuriating. He had an I-told-you-so smirk the rest of the day.

Chapter XI

JUST A FEW days before we left to go down to Miami to see Donna Repo and her mother, we tried the board once again for any additional material. If it was Don on the board, he was in a playful mood. We were getting used to this now. His sense of humor was a distinct characteristic. John had heard from Don's former crewmates that this was true, but he would check it out further with his family. If verified, it would add a bit of evidence to the already growing possibility that we were in contact with him.

The messages came fast and they were comical. They gave us the feeling that he was happy we were going to see his family. He even told a couple of unprintable airline jokes. One message really startled us: TUBBY IS LOT LUCKY BET IN THE FIFTH AT HIALEAH TRACK IN MIAMI TODAY BYE.

Beyond the fact that we had heard of Hialeah, neither John nor I knew anything about horse racing. And we weren't interested. We dismissed the message as another one of Don's jokes, and left it at that. When we left for Florida, the only thing we had on our minds was the growing importance of the story as very real evidence that we lived after death.

The atmosphere of the room in the Marriott Hotel at the Miami airport was a little strained. Donna was sitting in the chair closest to the door. She was statuesque, with a finely sculptured face. Mrs. Repo was in the other corner. She was delicate and appealing. Both women had a quiet warmth. John and I were sitting opposite them. There was a small table separating us. I think the anticipation of this meeting had made us all nervous wrecks. I had never before seen John more tense.

I sensed that Donna was somewhat apprehensive. I really couldn't blame her. I would have been equally wary. Neither Donna nor her mother knew exactly why we were there. John and I had very little to go on, other than that Alice had read one of John's books and liked it. I was hoping that Donna might relate to me, because we shared a common occupation. However, John was talking so much I could hardly get anything in. Usually in interviews, John did most of the listening, but this time he had a captive audience. He began telling Alice and Donna about a couple of his books. But one book led to another, and he eventually wound up talking about everything from the savannas of the African Sudan to the dangers of nuclear proliferation. All of it in unnecessarily meticulous detail.

The situation was indeed strange. Here we were intruding into a delicate and tragic incident. The last thing John or I wanted to do was to remind Alice and Donna of their grief. Yet by our mere presence, we would have to evoke some unpleasant memories of that fatal night. The main thrust of John's upcoming book was not the crash. It was the possibility of life being continuous. We were both beginning to believe that his book would transcend Alice,

Donna, Eastern Airlines, or any of us as individuals. It might point to a real existence somewhere else.

I knew what John was driving at through his lengthy book reviews. He wanted desperately to establish his credibility. In between African rats and plutonium, he filtered in information about his down-to-earth documentary films. Fuller was turning into a well-meaning but crashing bore.

Finally he said that this Eastern story really had him baffled. He told the Repos how he first heard of it on Scandinavian Airlines. How he began researching it. How qualified observers, like pilots, persistently reported such events. But what John failed to tell the Repos was *what* it was that he had first heard of. *What* it was that he had been researching. What the events *were* that the highly qualified observers were reporting.

John finally ended the elusive synopsis of his research by firmly stating that from the quality of the reports, and from the crew members we had talked to, there was no question in his mind that something serious was going on. But once again John failed to clue Alice and Donna in to what that serious thing was. I didn't know what to do, and I certainly wasn't going to volunteer any information. I just kept looking at John, and nodding in firm agreement.

I'm sure the Repos were totally confused. Neither one of us wanted to be the first to confront them with this incredible story.

John appeared to have ended his sincere but fuzzy explanation. With great composure and a friendly smile, Donna directly asked, "You mean the reports of my father reappearing on the L-1011s?"

It was as if she had heard the stories a hundred times before. She didn't appear to be upset. Her mother looked equally unperturbed. I was so relieved, now the point that John had tried to make was brought out into the open. I was also relieved to see Donna and her mother so composed.

Donna volunteered that she had heard the stories. But she had heard them all indirectly. Her fellow crew members were careful never to discuss her father's reappearances in front of her. They were just protecting her. Donna told us that she would not be opposed to hearing more about them. So far, her crewmates had mentioned very little.

Donna went on to say that when she first heard the stories, she had discounted them. But the persistence of the reports confused her. She couldn't imagine why so many crew members would want to make up something like this.

Donna claimed to be a realist. In addition to being a flight attendant, she was also a registered nurse. She was married to a pilot. They were both technical people, she said, and both found it very difficult to accept ghosts. On the other hand, she added: "This kind of thing sounds *exactly* like something my father would do." And then she laughed. While she had no morbid sentimentality, it was also evident that her love for her father had not faded.

Alice, too, spoke of Don not with sadness, but with love and affection. She told us that Don lived every day as if it were his last. They had been married twenty-nine years, and she never once had heard him say, "I wish I could have done that." He just did it, she said. When Don had his vacation, Alice said, they always packed the kids up and took them along. Regardless of where they went, they all went as a family. After Alice reminisced with us about Don, his joking and happy-go-lucky attitude, she shared with us some very personal experiences she had had since he died.

"One night I was sleeping and smelled this very strong odor of Vitalis on the pillow," she said. "That was what he used on his hair. He used it for years and years. But I was sleeping, and that smell actually woke me up. At first I thought maybe it was coming from a pillowcase I hadn't used for a long time. But I had bought all new pillows and pillowcases. So there couldn't have been any tonic on them. I just couldn't believe it. It was so strong. It stayed there for a long time.

"Then another time," she continued, "I just felt that he was right there in bed with me. It wasn't a dream. I was just so aware that he was there. I said I don't believe it. It can't be you. I said let me feel your hands. I felt his wedding band. I could feel the dent he had in his ring. I said, I know it's you. Yet, I was skeptical. I thought this just can't be."

Alice told us of many other incidents like this, all of them poignant. Listening to Alice tell of her various experiences with Don made me think back to what Laura Britebarth had said the first night I met her. She had said that she sensed that Don Repo wanted his wife to know of our investigation, and that Mrs. Repo would be receptive. Neither John nor I believed Laura at that time. Especially when she went on to tell us that Don Repo would be with us, and continue to help on the research for the book. Just months earlier those statements from Laura were enough to drive John up a wall. They probably still did. But could there be a chance she had been right?

I knew what was going through John's head. Should we tell Donna and Alice about our messages? We had agreed on the way down to Miami that we would only bring it up if they appeared open to the possibility of Don's communicating.

John laughed rather nervously, looked directly at Alice, and he said he had a *really* crazy question for her. Then he pulled out the transcripts from his briefcase. He stumbled over his words, then asked her if she ever had any trouble with mice in some sort of "family closet."

Alice just looked over at Donna and they both looked over at us. Alice then said that a couple of months earlier, they had mice in the attic. The attic was above their family room. The mice had been there for some months until her son John came home from college and set traps. The strange part was that the only way they could get to the attic was through what they called the family-room closet.

To use an old cliché, Fuller's jaw dropped visibly. But before John told her where we got the information, he said he had just a few more somewhat cryptic questions. He referred again to his typed transcripts of Don's "messages." He asked whether Don had anything to do with "pennies in their boy's room." Our message had read: TO GO INTO WASTE BASKET PENNIES SIT THERE BOYS ROOM.

Again, Donna and Alice looked startled. Alice told us that Don used to save pennies. After he died, they moved his small barrelful of pennies into their son John's room. In fact they still continued to add to the collection.

There comes a point every once in a while when even the strongest expression of surprise is not adequate. This was one of those times. John and I sat there silently. Both of us were dumbfounded.

"Sassy" was another strange word that had come over to us. It was the answer we had received when we first asked for Mrs. Repo's first name. Not until later did Alice recall that "Sassy" was the nickname Don had given her one time when she had started to put on a little weight.

The three messages that were such a puzzle to us, made sense to the Repos. I couldn't help but think back to the first time I had met John on that flight to Edmonton. I thought about the girls in the galley discussing the "writer" who was doing a jet-age legend. I thought about how I had offered to help with any research. I thought about all the events that had led up to our final confrontation with Alice and Donna.

And here we were now, all because of some messages that came over that crazy slab of wood, or whatever it was made of: CALL DONNA. John claimed to have written to Donna on impulse. But now I was wondering if impulses at some point cease to be impulses, just as coincidences cease to be coincidences. I was fast becoming convinced that we were being benevolently manipulated by the protagonist of this jet-age legend.

If those messages hadn't all checked out, I'm sure that John would not have had the nerve to tell Donna and Alice about our experiments. As it turned out, those rather trivial messages had a profound effect on them, as well as us. Alice and Donna were curious to know more about the Ouija board, and how the thing worked.

For some reason while I had been packing to go down to Miami, I had decided to bring the Ouija board along. John at first argued that it was a ridiculous idea, but I had followed my gut reaction and packed it anyway. Since Alice and Donna were interested in learning how the messages came over that strange board, I talked John into going down to the car and bringing it up for a brief demonstration.

John hesitantly sat down at the board with me, and we began to try to "call in" Don. I was scared to death it wouldn't work. But almost immediately, it began moving again in those same large circles. It soon began to spell out the answer to our questions:

Q. Don, are you there?
A. DON

Q. Don, who is here with us now?
A. ALICE

Alice and Donna looked perplexed, as they watched us ask the board questions. John and I were both embarrassed. Here we were, two grown people, confusing these women by not having the courage to tell them exactly what we were researching. We ask them rather unusual questions, and then we tell them that we got that information off a Ouija board, which we happened to have with us. Finally, we have the nerve to sit there and talk to the toy in front of them:

Q. Are there any special messages?
A. ALICE IS HERE LOVE HER JUST YOU ALICE
   FOR WIFE LOVE

At this point I sheepishly asked Alice and Donna if they would like to try the board. They said yes. Donna began by asking a question:

Q. Dad, did you know I was recently married?

A. YES I KNOW WORK HARD LOVE ALIVE TO JUST YOU WIFE LOVE YOU

Q. Have you any messages for my sister, Dad?

A. HOW ARE YOU MY SPECIAL DAUGHTER KISS ALISON FOR ME DEAR ALICE I LOVE YOU

The board was moving just as swiftly as it did for John and me. I was taking the letters down as Donna called them out. I felt that same presence of Don. It was as if he were standing in the room with us. Donna said that she felt as if her father were standing over her shoulder directing the indicator. It was the same feeling we had many times when we used the board.

Something was going on that defied all rational explanation, and yet it was as real as the room we were sitting in. Alice asked the next question:

Q. Don, is there any other message?

A. ALICE NORKO REPO I LOVE YOU NEVER FORGET PLEASE I LOVE YOU GOODNIGHT

The communications had ended as quickly and succinctly as they started. Alice and Donna were visibly touched. We all were. Alice told us that Norko was her maiden name. There was no longer doubt in their minds that our messages were from Don.

Alice, Donna, and I all had tears in our eyes as we walked to the hotel restaurant. I wasn't sure, but I thought I saw John flicking some dampness out of the corners of his. Although John didn't say anything, on the way out of the room he grabbed my hand and gently squeezed. I took this as a gesture of his belief.

After we said goodbye to the Repos, John and I had an after-dinner drink by the pool. The meeting with the Repos was now over and John was more relaxed. We were both relieved that it turned out to be a warm and comforting evening. Mrs. Repo and Donna were not only receptive to our research, they left sharing the same experiences that motivated us to get in touch with them in the first place. The dinner turned out to be more like a family reunion than the awkward and embarrasssing situation we had feared. During the dinner we talked about Don, his vivid sense of humor, and his love of life. We all even felt that maybe in some way he was right there with us. In fact, it might just possibly have been his influence that brought us together. At least, that's what I was thinking.

Several months later the manuscript of *The Ghost of Flight 401* was completed and John was waiting for editorial comments. It wasn't until after our meeting with the Repos that John decided to change the slant of his book from an impersonal to a personal story, from an investigation of a legend to an exploration of a distinct possibility. Although he never really came out and admitted that he believed 100 percent in our communications, somehow I just knew that Don Repo had gotten to him. And was continuing to get to him in some very unusual ways.

The following Sunday, we were having breakfast at Oscar's Deli in Westport. John picked up a *New*

York Times from a large stack on the floor, and brought it back to our small table. He put the thick Sunday paper on his lap, and began to lift up the numerous divided sections to find the book review. He got midway through the paper, and suddenly stopped. He leaned down and looked at something. I thought he had come across a review of one of his own books. After several seconds, he pointed it out to me.

It was the front page of the travel section. It consisted of almost a full-page, half-tone of the flight deck of a modern plane. The picture was taken over the shoulders of the pilot and co-pilot. The pilot was turned halfway around, facing the camera. Nearly all the instrument panel was clearly visible behind him. Lying flat on that panel was a *real*, bright, shiny penny. It was not in the picture. It was *there*. On the paper.

I was as surprised as John to find a brand-new penny just sitting there. My first impulse was to think of that penny as a good omen. I was about to reach over and pick it up, and make a wish. Then it hit me. I told John to just look at that paper. Look at where that penny was.

It was in the picture of the cockpit of an airplane. The penny was lying on the picture of that panel in the same relative position as the landing-gear signal light. And the landing-gear light had been the indirect cause of the crash of Flight 401. We both thought that was awfully peculiar, but we went on to eat our breakfast. We thought nothing more of it.

At least we thought nothing more about it until we got back home. I suddenly remembered the message we had received from Don Repo about the penny and the paper. About a penny and the *New*

York Times, as a matter of fact. It had been some months earlier. I couldn't recall what the exact message was, or why it had been given to us on that ridiculous toy.

I went into John's office and got out the transcripts. I began to read them. I came across the message that absolutely floored me.

Q. Can you give us further proof?
A. READ NY TIMES PENNY WILL FIND THERE

I had asked Don for further proof, after my gold ring had broken. That's when Don had given us that apparent message. But when I had gone to look at the *New York Times,* and couldn't find any penny, John and I had just chalked it up as another one of Don's playful jokes. At least, until now. I couldn't wait to show John what I had discovered.

John was in the other room. I took the penny-message transcripts in to him, without saying anything.

Then I asked him: "Just read the first question on the top of the page." He did.

His only comment was, "Well, I'll be damned."

We both went through the *Times* again for that picture on the front of the travel section. We carefully studied the illustration. The pilot looking back over his shoulder. The control panel behind him.

The penny had been in the same location as the faulty landing-gear, or nose-wheel warning light. There was no question in my mind now that our communications had been real. This time, even John didn't say that it was just a coincidence. He just said, "I'll be damned, " for a second time.

I figured his "I'll be damned" lay halfway between "Knock it off" and "Holy cow." For Fuller, that was pretty good.

That penny message hounded me the rest of the day. I couldn't shake the feeling that this story was growing more important with every piece of evidence that came in.

I asked John if he would consider adding to his book the incidents of my ring breaking, and now this penny-on-the-paper thing. He overreacted to my question. He carried on about how he was scared to death right now. So much so, he felt he was going to lose all his credibility. I decided it was better to drop the issue.

Then I thought: Wait a minute. What had that strange message about "Tubby" and "Hialeah" meant?

My memory was a little vague. Again I dug out the transcripts of our sessions. I ran through them quickly. I suddenly found it. TUBBY IS LOT LUCKY BET IN THE FIFTH AT HIALEAH TRACK IN MIAMI TODAY BYE, it read.

An idea struck me. What if a horse named Tubby had been running at Hialeah at that time? I checked the date of the transcript. It was March 2, 1976. It was highly unlikely, I realized, that there even was a horse named "Tubby." However, whether Tubby won or not on that day was really unimportant. If there was a horse by that name running anywhere in Florida at that time, it would be a very interesting piece of evidence. I was wondering what Fuller would say then.

I had talked to Laura in New York a few days earlier. She had mentioned that she was going down to Miami for a long weekend. Maybe she could do some research on Tubby while she was down there.

I didn't have the faintest idea as to where to tell her to begin checking. Maybe the newspaper files. Maybe some kind of racing sheet down there. I knew absolutely nothing about horseracing. Laura thought my request was very amusing. She agreed to find out whatever she could.

That weekend Laura called us from Miami. She asked us if we were sitting down. Then she told me that there *was* a horse named Tubby, and that it *was* running at that time in Hialeah, during February and March 1976. His full name was Tubby Applegate. He was called Tubby for short. He was a four-year-old chestnut gelding. His father was named Third Martini. His mother was Sue Saint Marie. His owner then was W.H. Chamberlain. His trainer was H.A. Jerkins. He came in second in the second race on January 24, winning a $600 purse. He came in first in the seventh race on February 25, with a purse of $5,525. On March 3, the first chance we would have had to act on this ethereal tip, he was running in the fifth, just as the message from Don Repo announced.

Don had goofed only in one regard—Tubby did *not* finish in the money. He failed to take any purse. But how in the world this information came through was something I could never in a million years understand.

I passed the information along to John. The only thing he said was: "Oh, boy." He repeated it. "Oh, boy." Just like that.

This was enough to throw him, but again he refused to use this information in his book. He needed to have witnesses outside the two of us—and no one had been around to check it.

The communication didn't end with TUBBY,

GOLD RING, or PENNY ON TIMES. Our very last message was after the book went to press. John and I decided to ask Don if he knew the story was completed. He apparently not only knew, but hadn't lost his sense of humor: SO SORRY BOOK NOW OVER HOW ABOUT ANOTHER STAR ROLE FOR REPO BUB.

We somehow had the feeling that after the book was written our communications with Don would end. We asked where he was going, and what he was doing over there. The reply was: WAIT AND SEE. When we pressed him for an answer, the letters spelled: GO TO STORE BUY SOME BEER HA HA HA GOODBYE.

We have tried occasionally to get further messages, but they have been muddy and confused. The link seems to have been broken. Although the communications appear to have ended, the story will live on in our hearts. I don't think either one of us will ever thoroughly understand how and why all this happened, but there are lots of things that we will never adequately understand with our three-dimensional thinking. This is just one of that kind of thing that belongs to faith. I would now be satisfied with just that. John, I don't think, would ever really be completely satisfied, but it was necessary for him to look at these last months in a different, more analytical way. John would continue to be overly cautious, afraid of being taken for a sucker, and constantly suspicious.

Three years have passed since I first met John on the flight to Edmonton, and began researching the story of 401. The research led to my psychic development. The psychic development led us out of this conventionally confined landscape into a new, less defined type of real estate. I wasn't sure exactly what would happen to my psychic ability after the ghost book was completed. I kept thinking that maybe it would just disappear as fast as it appeared. Both John and I felt a deep sense of loss after our communications with Don had ended. I still don't belong to any organized religious group. John and I sort of try them all, building our own do-it-yourself kit. We try to find a little bit of truth everywhere we go. Don helped me to see that nothing is ever really black or white. There are gradations. You don't have to believe in anything totally. You can accept and reject as it suits your belief system. Trivial things in my life that were important to me before the research, have been put back in their proper perspective. Most important, through the research, I have learned how to get out of myself, and see a much larger picture of life.

What happened after happily-ever-after? I quit flying. John and I got married. Now we both share that little green hut on the river. Fuller only occasionally gets on my nerves, as I do his, but together our horizons have widened and our sense of wonderment at the universe has increased. I have not lost that ability to go back into that higher self or seek my "Spiritual Society" for guidance and insight. I like to think that I have been able to help not only myself, but some friends as well through this psychic and spiritual channel.

Things happen in strange ways. I was content to know very little about the vast and unexplored areas of the mind. I was not searching for anything, especially mediumship. Now I would feel so empty and alone without this new sense of awareness! I am not unique. I'm convinced that we all have an ability to develop this awareness to a greater or lesser degree.

I can't say my life has changed drastically, but I can say it has improved. I have a better understanding of what I am here for and the direction in which I am going. I have added a whole new dimension to my life by accident—or was it an accident?

EPILOGUE
by John G. Fuller

I HADN'T A thought in the world when I asked Elizabeth to do some free-lance research for me on the story of Flight 401 that she would turn out to be a psychic herself. I know she didn't, either. She was enthusiastic, interested, and liked to talk to people. She was as curious about these stories of the Eastern "ghost" as I was. She had already heard secondhand versions of them from dozens of airline crews, and the idea of researching them as a sort of detective intrigued her. Not only that, she could get paid for the research on the reasonably anemic free-lance scale that I was able to pay her. Because her airline put into many ramps that shared the same facilities as Eastern, she would be in a position to chat informally with Eastern crews to learn more about this strange story.

At the start, I had been convinced that it was a modern myth, legend, or ghost story—whatever you wanted to call it—and I felt it would be interesting to see how such a latter-day "Flying Dutchman" tale generated itself into a story that practically every crew member on almost any airline knew about.

Elizabeth made an ideal research assistant, even though her first reports were filed somewhat informally on airsick bags. Her knack at getting people to open up was nothing short of miraculous, and she wasn't at all a psychic research buff and knew little about the field. This was important, because I didn't want a researcher who was interested in selling the supernormal, or who would get carried away with the stories she heard.

She also had a great sense of humor, and could laugh at herself. Anyone who could fall asleep in an overhead rack had to have a good sense of humor, and certainly would be fundamentally un-psychic or she would have been forewarned not to doze off.

It was a strange thing to watch this unbelievable talent and capacity grow right in front of my eyes. From the moment she began rattling off names neither of us had heard before, through the sessions with that ridiculous but obviously operational Ouija board, I tried to explain everything either as a coincidence or a reflection of the unconscious mind. But there comes a time with this sort of thing when you can no longer explain things away, even though you want to. The so-called rational explanations simply don't come off.

On the other hand, it's almost impossible to accept the irrational explanations. So you are left in midair, wondering what the hell is up. This is what happened with the 401 story, and I will defy anyone to go through the same experiences we did and not come up with a big question mark that has to tilt in the direction of what some people call the irrational and others call the supernormal. My inclination is to call it a "sensory-extension syndrome" which needs a lot more openminded investigation than it's getting from objective observers who don't have any axe to grind in either direction.

From the time the Flight 401 book was finished, I've watched Elizabeth put to use this sensory-extension syndrome of hers in everyday life. We drove over 9,000 miles through Europe working on several stories for *The Reader's Digest* the following summer, and I must say there was some very practical value to Elizabeth's talent.

At one point it was necessary for us to meet a friend arriving by train at Hilversum, Holland, from Amsterdam. Hilversum is quite a large city, with a labyrinth of streets that must have been laid out by a herd of cattle. We were a little late driving into the city, and had no idea at all where the railroad station was. We found ourselves in a residential section of large homes, and there was no one around to ask directions. We finally found one lady wheeling a baby carriage, but she couldn't speak English, and time was getting tighter all the while.

Elizabeth said: "Look—I might as well try to go into an altered state of consciousness, and see if I can get anything."

By this time, I was willing to do anything, so I told her to go ahead. I was sure it would be fruitless, but I had been wrong before.

Elizabeth half-closed her eyes, and then said: "Go straight ahead. There's a traffic light about a mile and a half from here. The only traffic light."

If there was a traffic light, there was no sign of it, even though this street was broad and stretched straight ahead. However, I kept driving.

"When you get to the light," she continued, "then make a right turn."

My hopes were fading, but I said, "Then what?"

"Then," she said, "go exactly six-tenths of a mile. Six-tenths of a mile. Then make another right."

Elizabeth Fuller

This was getting more ridiculous all the time. How could any "Spiritual Society" or anyone else judge a distance with that mathematical precision? But just about this point, I saw the traffic light looming ahead. That was at least encouraging. There were still no people around to ask on the streets or sidewalks.

We got to the traffic light, and I turned right, checking the speedometer as I did so. It was calibrated in miles, rather than kilometers, so I could check this ridiculous six-tenths of a mile. "What are we supposed to do after that?" I asked.

"We are to turn right again, as I told you."

"Then what?"

"Drive for three blocks," she said, with her eyes still half-closed. "Then, ahead and on the right, you will see a rather tall building. On top of it, there is a very large sign that reads: GARAGE. The railroad station will be just in front of that building."

I knew we were wrong now. The word "garage" didn't seem to be in common use in Holland—if at all. Poor Elizabeth had let her imagination run away with her Spiritual Society.

I looked at the speedometer, and it read exactly six-tenths of a mile from our traffic-light checkpoint. On the right, there was a nondescript street. It looked almost as if we were on an alley or a dead-end street. I took it anyway, desperate now because of the lateness of the hour. There were trees on the road, and not much visible ahead.

But when we had gone two blocks, we could see clearly. There was a large building on the right. On top of it was a large sign reading: GARAGE, in two-feet-high letters. Just across the street from it was the railroad station. I was literally stunned.

It was just about the first time that Elizabeth had ever given me the right directions to anywhere.

One time in Holland, we were driving to meet a retired police commissioner at his country home. Elizabeth described the home exactly, an hour before we arrived there. But she said two things that were rather unusual. One was that she saw a very old woman in the house, and the other was she clearly saw an unrepaired broken window in an otherwise impeccable home.

We arrived there to find the house exactly as Elizabeth had described it, in color, shape, size, and detail. Soon after our arrival, we found that there was a ninety-year-old lady who lived in sort of a private apartment on the first floor. But there was no sign whatever of an unrepaired broken window. Judging from the meticulous Dutch care with which the house was kept, this would be unlikely.

Before we left, I told the commissioner and his wife of the accurate description Elizabeth had given of the house, and told how she had missed completely in only one item: the broken window.

The commissioner laughed, and said: "You didn't look behind the sofa where you were sitting. There is a broken windowpane there that we haven't had a chance to get repaired."

Things like this would happen all the time on that research trip through Europe. Without a map, Elizabeth got us from the outskirts of Paris to a hotel on the Left Bank we had never been to, simply by stating when to turn right and when to turn left— or even when to take an angled street. She was better than radar.

More serious are the séances and readings that Elizabeth has cautiously experimented with. She continues to "get through" names, dates, places, and events that are so specific they can only be explained by extended telepathy or by palpable evidence of communication with those who have died. Either of these explanations is pretty wild, but I know of no others. "Extended telepathy" would have to mean that someone would have to send a nonelectronic communication to Elizabeth's brain which would enable her to come up with information about the life of a deceased that even the relative involved often doesn't know.

A good example of this happened when Elizabeth experimented with a séance at the home of a former editor of one of the most sophisticated magazines in the United States. Elizabeth came through with facts about a man in uniform who was killed over the China Sea, and who trained at Pensacola, Florida, as a pilot. His sister's name was Catherine. He had a curly-headed child of about four, and had lived on the West Coast. He had gone to a Catholic University in the Midwest, and had belonged to a church called St. Anthony's. He seemed happy that his wife had now married his best friend.

While all this information was coming across, no one in the room said anything to confirm or deny these details. When the flow stopped, the editor confirmed that he had a nephew he was very fond of, who had been shot down in the Vietnam War in the China Sea. The nephew had gone to Marquette University, lived on the West Coast, had a sister named Catherine, and a curly-headed child of four. His parish was St. Anthony's. His wife had recently been remarried, to the pilot's best friend.

But no one was sure about Pensacola. Finally, someone went upstairs, dug up a book of clippings, and brought it downstairs. The first clipping in the book had a picture of the Navy pilot, with a caption that confirmed he had trained at Pensacola.

Again, Elizabeth has repeated this sort of thing dozens of times. In Geneva, she was persuaded to give a reading to a lady neither of us had ever seen before in our lives. She received confirmed information about the woman's deceased husband, from his name and when and how he had died, to a trophy consisting of crossed skis, engraved with the year "1946."

In spite of all this, Elizabeth is the easiest person in the world to live with. None of this has spoiled her fantastic sense of humor nor her down-to-earth practicality. Of course, I can't get away with anything—but then I don't particularly want to, and it would be no good if I did. She can pinpoint what I'm thinking or doing from a room in the other part of the house. I keep saying to myself: *Thank God I'm a man of reasonably pure thoughts.*

When I try to get Elizabeth to explain just what in the hell goes on when she gets this kind of information, she irritates me. One time I pressed hard for an explanation, and she said: "I just see things like a mental image in my mind's eye. It sort of rolls out on my mind as if it's a dream, only it's not quite like that."

I said: "That's the vaguest story I've ever run across. Can't you do better than that?"

"Well, it's sort of like I'm compelled to say something," she answered. "It's like a strong hunch, as if they've told it to me earlier."

"But what about when you seem to be getting messages from someone who has died? What happens then?"

"I just feel as if—it's hard to say, love. I can't explain it, I really can't. Other than what I just said."

"Yes, but what you just said is too vague."

"I can't help it," she answered, with one of her sweeter smiles. "I told you, love, I can't tell you any more."

"All right. Take just one thing. Take that 1946 trophy with the crossed skis. What about that?"

"Well, it was as if I just *knew*. It's like when you listen to somebody telling you about something he did. Like climb the Matterhorn. You evoke visual images, or something triggers a picture inside you. With the trophy, something triggered this image, something beyond all of us in the room, beyond experiences I could relate to—I saw something that I had never seen before, and I knew it was a communication, because it was nothing I could relate to anything in the rest of my life. You not only see or hear things, you *feel* something is right. Without any rational explanation, you can just *feel* something is right."

"Don't you feel sort of silly, blurting out these rather wild and disconnected facts—at least at the time you say them?" I asked.

"Afterward, I say: *Wow. I don't know where I got the nerve to say all that stuff.* But while it's happening, emotionally, I have sort of given myself up to this higher self."

I had noticed that at some of these séances Elizabeth will suddenly come out with statements that would sound ridiculous if they didn't actually apply to the case at hand. I always have the feeling that she's going to fail, and I feel embarrassed for her, but almost inevitably, it all comes together and is confirmed.

What Elizabeth and I are both gratified by is the number of letters, including many from airline pilots, that have come in since *The Ghost of Flight 401* was published. They almost universally indicate that the story of Don Repo has given them a sense of peace and calm about the usually grisly subject of death and dying. Elizabeth and I both feel the same way.

I have a bad habit of constantly trying to hide my emotions. I'm usually successful, which may be good or bad. But following through on the story of Don Repo and watching Elizabeth develop her expanded sense of awareness—without losing her sense of humor or sense of reality—have considerably changed my outlook. For the first time, I now believe there is strong evidence that there is such a thing as an afterlife, and that it's a very real and tangible one.

Many people have asked us whether this isn't in conflict with conventional religions. I can't help feeling that it is just the opposite; it serves as a solid platform for any belief, whether it's Christianity, Judaism, or the Muslim, Hindu, Buddhist or other of the world's great faiths. Rational and objective evidence of an afterlife simply complements the beliefs that have been accepted on faith.

Since the modern, materialistic, scientific age swept in, we've been exposed to a rationalist vocabulary that has put a heavy strain on the poetic language of the scriptures and mystical writings. If belief in life after death can be framed in modern, rationalist diction, it simply brings new life to the old scriptures. It reinforces them. It complements them. It renews them with fresh vigor. It can bring back faith that has faltered with the onslaught of total materialism. This, we found, was the theory of the Spiritual Frontiers Fellowship, which has blended the rational aspects of the paranormal with orthodox religion. In other words, they have found no conflict here, only verification.

Evidence, of course, is not proof. Elizabeth and I want to follow up more on this, and see where the evidence leads. It won't be an easy job, but there couldn't be a more interesting adventure story.